T0339707

DOCTORS WITHOUT BORDERS
IN ETHIOPIA:

AMONG THE AFAR

Doctors Without Borders In Ethiopia: Among the Afar

Nyla Jo Jones Hubbard

Algora Publishing
New York

Library of Congress Cataloging-in-Publication Data —

Hubbard, Nyla Jo Jones.
    Doctors without Borders in Ethiopia: Among the Afar/ Nyla Jo Jones
Hubbard.
        p. ; cm.
    Includes index.
    ISBN 978-0-87586-852-3 (soft: alk. paper)—ISBN 978-0-87586-853-0 (hard:
alk. paper)—ISBN 978-0-87586-854-7 (ebook) 1. Médecins sans frontières
(Association)—Biography. 2. Voluntary Health Agencies—Ethiopia—
Biography. 3. Volunteers—Ethiopia—Biography. I. Title.
    [DNLM: 1. Médecins sans frontières (Association) 2. Voluntary Health
Agencies--Ethiopia--Autobiography. 3.   Laboratory Personnel--Ethiopia--
Autobiography. 4. Voluntary Workers--Ethiopia--Autobiography. WA 1]
    RA552.E8H83 2011
    362.10963—dc22

                                2010051137

    Front Cover: Ethiopia - Ethiopians peer through a hole in a fence while
waiting in line for food and medicine at a clinic run by Médecins sans frontières
(MSF) (Doctors Without Borders) in the town of Kuyera, 250kms south of
Addis Ababa, Ethiopia, 01 October 2008.
    © Stephen Morrison/epa/Corbis

Printed in the United States

Dedicated to my team, expat and Afar, and to Hawah Kamara, my MSF USA contact, who died in 2005. She was the warmth of Africa personified.

"I pray thee, then. Write me as one who loves his fellow men."
—from *Abou Ben Adhem* by Leigh Hunt

TABLE OF CONTENTS

Table of Contents

Preface: Signing Up for a Life Without Borders

Friends have asked, "Whatever possessed you to go to Ethiopia?"
These things develop.

In part, it was frustration with the whole US medical system. I'm a Medical Technologist (recently renamed Medical Laboratory Scientist), and have worked in the clinical laboratory for over 35 years. Many of the tests I run are "CYA medicine," not ordered because the patient needs them but because the doctor doesn't want any lawyer to be able to ask in the future "Doctor, given the patient's diagnosis (which, of course, hadn't been made at the time), shouldn't you have ordered a __?," then going on to name some esoteric test which may not, in fact, have aided in the diagnosis or altered the outcome for the patient but which surely would have driven up the cost of care. All of us would like to feel that our work is pertinent and to get some feedback when our tests make a difference in the treatment of the patient. Gone is the day when a lab tech routinely visited the ward to draw blood. The lab is far separated now from that bedside. We seldom see a patient, and positive feedback is hard to come by.

Then there's family creed. I was raised and remain Quaker. The idea of service is not preached so much as it is absorbed. The family of my great-great grandmother was active in the Underground Railroad in

Indiana and my great-aunt went to West Virginia after she graduated from nursing school in the early 1900s to work with the coal miners there. Generations of do-gooders make their mark.

As a girl, I wanted to be a nurse like my great-aunt, but there was no money for me to go to school. I married young and already had a two-year-old child when I heard about a program that would allow a person to work his or her way through basic lab training. It took two years to qualify for my technician's license that way, when a year would have done it in a school program, but I did get the license and eventually went on to college. The laboratory profession has a hierarchy in the US much as nursing does. At that time it was technician, technologist and supervisor. The state of Florida tested and licensed lab personnel. I was eventually licensed as a supervisor but I wanted to be Medicare approved and, at that time, Medicare regulations required a laboratory supervisor to have a Baccalaureate degree. It took me seventeen years to get my bachelor's degree which I obtained at the age of 45. In 1994 I took the ASCP exam for national registry and achieved what is generally considered to be the most prestigious of the lab designations, MT, ASCP (Medical Technologist, American Society of Clinical Pathologists). That girl who washed the lab glassware to pay her way and raised two kids while juggling daycare finally had letters after her name.

However, I didn't want to go with any group associated with religion. I had seen the destructive effects of evangelism in Peru and I was not in the business of uprooting culture to save souls. I remember seeing the news when Doctors without Borders, known as Médecins *sans Frontières*, or MSF, in the rest of the world, received the Nobel Peace Prize in 1999. I watched the televised medical staff moving from one sufferer to another, addressing real need. Not a single patient in the video appeared robust. I imagined what it would be like to work in an area where the primary causes of death were AIDs, malaria and TB as opposed to the top killers in the US: heart disease, cancer and stroke. Tests have changed over the years but I have been helping to diagnose and monitor those same three diseases in this country for thirty-seven years and one underlying cause for the ailments has not changed. Americans are overfed and under exercised.

I still had obligations in 1999, but time passed and, at the age of fifty-five, it suddenly occurred to me that I was free. My family was grown, my marriage was over and my expenses were few. It still didn't happen immediately, as the website for Doctors without Borders/MSF did not mention the need for techs. While I was staining slides for TB at the hospital where I worked in Florida the idea came again. TB was listed on the website as one of the biggest health problems, so who was examining the slides? I went back to the website and clicked on "Urgent Needs" and what popped up but "Lab Techs"!

I applied online and received a call in April 2001 from the MSF headquarters in New York, asking me to come for an interview. It seemed that the interview went well. They were all pleased to get a tech and it was just the next month when Laurence Bonte, the laboratory technician in charge of laboratories for MSF France, called me. She asked if I would be willing to serve in a TB clinic in a desert region of Ethiopia for six months. Since I had spent many years living without air conditioning in Florida, I thought I was prepared for heat. Also, I did know that Ethiopia has over seven hundred species of birds, a big plus for an avid birder like me.

As fate would have it, I met a man who would catch my interest five weeks before I left for mission when Merle Hubbard joined us on an Audubon field trip. He e-mailed me later with an invitation to dinner. The five-week time limit is probably the reason our relationship began, as it meant that I had no fear. I viewed it as a pleasant interlude while I waited to go to Ethiopia.

Chapter 1. Ethiopia and Doctors Without Borders

The Doctors Without Borders (MSF) is "an international humani-tarian aid organization that provides emergency medical assistance to populations in danger in more than seventy countries." Their mission statement goes on to explain, "In countries where health structures are insufficient or even nonexistent, MSF collaborates with authorities such as the Minister of Health to provide assistance. MSF works in rehabilitation of hospitals and dispensaries, in vaccination programs and water and sanitation projects. MSF also works in remote health care centers, slum areas and provides training of local personnel. All this is done with the objective of rebuilding health structures to ac-ceptable levels."

This paragraph condenses a world of effort and they accomplish their work with surprisingly little fanfare in the aftermath of war, fam-ine or natural disaster. For example MSF already had 792 volunteers in place in Haiti before the recent earthquake and Haiti was featured in their literature long before it made headlines after the quake. I had heard of them specifically only in the Nobel Prize announcement. Yet, Doctors without Borders/MSF is truly worldwide. There are twenty-four member nations and offices in nineteen countries. The mission to which I was assigned belonged to MSF France but was an "English-speaking mission," meaning all expat personnel would be expected to speak English regardless of nationality. The decision on what the official language will be is dependent on the language used in the host country. Though the Afar tribe with whom we would be working often spoke French, the secondary language used in the capital of Ethiopia was English. The two languages had both bases covered.

My flight plan included a stop in New York, so I decided to visit the United Nations. I was particularly interested in UNICEF. UNICEF, like Doctors without Borders (MSF), earns the top rating of four stars on the Charity Navigator website. However, UNICEF is dependent on government contributions for 64% of their funding. The US Congress just appropriated $134 million for UNICEF in 2011. In contrast MSF has not solicited or received any funding from the US government since 2002, and they limit government funding to less than 20% of their total funds raised. This allows MSF the freedom to criticize foreign aid practices that they find to be detrimental in the field. They also do not accept contributions from pharmaceutical or biotechnology companies nor from oil, gas, gold and diamond extractors, alcohol and tobacco industries, or arms manufacturers. MSF is able to speak out without biting the hand that feeds it.

I had only one day in the city before Hawah helped me get my luggage to the airport shuttle, gave me the three kisses on the cheek that is customary in much of Africa, and I arrived in Paris on the morning of May 23. The plane was an hour and a half late and getting through DeGaulle was a nightmare of too much luggage and no elevators. I mourned my lack of the French language when I couldn't understand the signs and hoped that it would not continue to be a problem.

Indeed everyone at the MSF headquarters in Paris did speak English. I arrived so late that I had missed some of my appointments. A French holiday occurred during my time there so I wound up in Paris for a few days, but there were many meetings. I was introduced to conditions at my mission, including an update on previous problems between staff. I then had a pep talk from a German girl living for many years in France. She gave me advice about the use of hand gestures, basically "don't" as the gesture may mean something entirely different in the host culture. She impressed upon me the adages, "Don't embarrass your home country. Don't embarrass MSF. Don't criticize their practices. You are a guest in their home." It was good advice.

The next day, there were forms to be signed for the deposit of the $600 per month that MSF would put into my bank account at home while I was away. I was also allowed a small stipend by MSF for food while on mission but it was never more than enough. I am not surprised that MSF continues to get four stars on the charity evaluator because at no time did I see people misusing funds.

If I had been responsible for a mortgage or other large financial commitment, I would probably not have been able to go on mission. Employers in the US healthcare system are not accustomed to giving employees time off for endeavors such as this one. I had to quit my job at the hospital in Florida because twelve weeks off was the most they could give me.

Laurence Bonte, who was in charge of laboratories for MSF France and who interviewed me initially, had me examine some slides under her supervision. The TB on the slides was familiar but I had only found malaria twice in thirty years in the US, both patients being travelers, and I had to get comfortable with the two kinds that are found in "my" area of Africa, P. Vivax and P. Falciparum.

I was then immunized for meningitis, typhoid and rabies. This was in addition to the vaccinations for Hepatitis A and Yellow Fever that I had before I left the States.

Between appointments, I met a logistician who had returned from Gahla. He gave me the real lowdown. There was no electricity except what could be produced with a generator and, with all supplies, including gasoline, having to be brought from Addis, it was used very sparingly. That made my hair dryer unnecessary. I shoved all non-essentials inside the big suitcase that I had lugged through the airport and left it in the closet at MSF headquarters.

Just before 5AM on May 26, I hauled my one bag and the mail bag down six flights of stairs. I had pared down my luggage but all volunteers are expected to take the mail bag. Mail is not sent directly to the area of mission but instead is funneled through Paris by volunteers headed for the host country. This is more dependable but it is also slower as no one may be coming to your area for quite some time.

With the mail, I had 35.6 kilos of luggage. The limit was 40 kilos. A taxi picked me up and I left Paris for Addis Ababa.

Getting into Africa

I was tired and toting heavy baggage when we arrived in Addis at 8:45PM where I couldn't find the person sent to fetch me. That was not surprising since the airport authority in Addis has always taken security seriously and no one who isn't a passenger is allowed into the airport or the immediate area outside arrivals. Later, I learned that the person was there but could not get my attention in the dark from the distant compound where greeters were required to wait. In the litera- ture sent to me, I had been told that, if no one was there to get me, not to pay more than $10.00 for a taxi. There was no lack of taxis, the driv- ers of which were all in my face. I asked who knew how to get to the MSF guest house, reading off the address. One elderly man assured me that he did. It was a long ride requiring four stops for directions before we found the house for MSF Belgium. Wrong MSF, but the officer of that branch knew the location for the guest house of MSF France and he was kind enough to leave an "end of mission" party to drive me there. The main surprise I had upon entering the guest house was the chill. The house was cool and damp. The blankets on the bed were unlike any I'd ever seen, thick and tightly woven with designs that went all the way through. After diligently weeding from my luggage all items not meant for a hot dry climate, I needed those blankets.

The MSF France guesthouse in Addis was decorated by the doc- tor who had established the mission in Gahla and who used the house when on breaks, along with anyone else who was on leave from mis- sion. There were two portraits, Che Guevara and Bob Marley. The fur- niture was of heavy dark wood and there was a definite Arab influence. The house, of cement block, was behind a wall as were the majority of houses in Addis. Most of the walls were topped with broken glass, presumably to deter the scaling of them but the glass was often colored and also served as decoration. This arrangement eliminated the need to lock house doors since the gate to the courtyard is locked.

On my first morning Veronique, the wife of the doctor who was the Medical Director of MSF Addis Ababa, came to get me and we went shopping for food which, by Western standards, was very inexpensive. Driving in Addis was like a game of bumper cars. The traffic lights did not work. It was strictly a "wait for your chance and don't be too timid to take it" situation and included competing with goats. People had their wares set up on the very edge of the roads and thought nothing of running out into traffic to try to sell them. Many roads were muddy; with puddles and potholes, since the rainy season in Addis was beginning. Added to this were the beggars, many beggars, some sitting on skate boards on the stumps of their legs. Many men were missing limbs; they were veterans of the Civil War with Eritrea. They had been forced to fight but there was no social system to take care of them after they were injured. The main culprit was land mines.

A report by the International Campaign to Ban Land Mines asserts that at least 1,266 people were killed by land mines and 3,891 were injured by them last year alone. Those are the reported injuries. Many sources estimate the actual human cost to be much higher. Landmine Monitor reports that 70-85% of these casualties are civilians, many of them women and children. The vast majority of these injuries do not occur during wartime. Land mines are still exploding that were planted during the First World War. According to Reuters Alert Net, April, 2007, the northern territories of Ethiopia, those bordering Eritrea, were so heavily mined as to endanger 442,000 people in the region after the Ethiopia/Eritrea conflict. The UN has funded removal of mines and to date, about eleven square kilometers have been cleared. It is said that is costs $3.00 to make a land mine but $1000.00 to clear one. Until and unless mines are cleared, civilians who normally reside in that area cannot return in safety to their homes. They can't safely farm the mined land or access water sources. Land mines hamper efforts of aid workers and the supply of provisions to victims. Ethiopia has signed the Mine Ban Treaty and reports that the government has not imported any land mines since the fall of the Soviet regime of Mengistu in 1991.

Though the US stopped using land mines in 1991 and stopped producing them in 1997, our military still has stockpiles of them in South Korea. Sixty-eight senators, well over the two thirds of the Senate needed to ratify, signed a letter to President Obama this year asking the administration to join the 1997 Mine Ban Treaty but the US has not agreed to sign. This means that, rather than siding with the eighty percent of the world's countries, including all of our NATO allies, in supporting the Land Mine Ban, the US government has chosen, along with China, Russia, Pakistan, Israel, Iran, both Koreas and others, to refuse to sign. Many of the countries refusing to sign still manufacture and sell land mines.

Addis is situated in the Ethiopian highlands, surrounded by verdant hills. The climate is moist and temperate and there was plenty of green.. There were modern buildings but there were also slums. The poverty was not unexpected. In the city of Iquitos, in the Amazon basin, I had seen the staring children, the overcrowding and the hopelessness. These people were a taller, darker version of the same want. There was evidence of industry, though; sprawling open air markets selling fruit, secondhand clothes and empty bags with US WHEAT stamped on them. There were tiny one-window store fronts on many blocks, just the proverbial hole in the wall with a tarp affixed above the window and a Fanta sign stuck on the cement, plugging soda and soap. Individuals had set up little tables on the corners selling small quantities of lentils and beans, perhaps a single day's supply, an indication of the way many of the people were obliged to live.

We saw women working on the roads, heavy work usually done in the US by men. At the time I was there, Addis Ababa was about half Ethiopian Orthodox Christian and about half Muslim. The Christian women wore shawls called natalas. They were made of a filmy muslin and bordered with tabibs (borders) of different, often intricate, designs. The Muslim women were obliged to cover their heads, though it didn't appear to be as diligently enforced as it is in some Muslim countries. All the women looked tired.

After shopping, we went to lunch at a pleasant place called Top View, well named as the location was overlooking the city. Veronique's little boy was with us. He did not speak English but hers was perfect. I soon learned that Veronique was a doctor herself, an OB/GYN(obstetrician/gynecologist), but she was not allowed to work in Ethiopia. The rule of the Ethiopian government was that only one member of an expat family could work. Since her husband was working, she couldn't. So, in that country, with the highest maternal death rate in the world, a specialist in that discipline was not allowed to work, even for free. For that reason, she and her husband were planning to return to France soon, a great loss.

Benito Mussolini invaded Ethiopia in 1935 and formally annexed the country in 1936 with the idea that the fertile highlands could be colonized by Italian farmers. This was a blow for the Ethiopians as they had, up to that point, been the only country in Africa that had never been colonized. Ethiopia contains the highest land on the continent giving the country the sobriquet of "the roof of Africa." The mountains and inaccessibility had served to keep Ethiopia free of outside conquerors and Mussolini's plans ended, too, with the defeat of the Axis in World War II. His legacy lives on, however, in the many pizza places in evidence and the pasta that is often eaten in Ethiopia.

At one point in our journey that first morning in Addis, Veronique and I passed under some arches with symbols reminiscent of Red Square. Although Ethiopia maintained peace for close to thirty years after the end of the Second World War and the subsequent return of Emperor Haile Selassie, the territory of Eritrea had long been considered an integral part of their nation, lost only during the Battle of Adwa (Italy's first major attempt on Ethopia) in 1896. Rulers especially wanted it back since it had been Ethiopia's only port. With the end of Italian rule, the British controlled Eritrea until 1962 when it was annexed to Ethiopia, but under conditions that prevented the evolution of a strong and unified country. Eritrea was predominantly Muslim and the rulers in Addis were Christian. Haile Selassie, though he tried to improve life for Ethiopians overall, had angered many by making Amharic the official language and confining most of the improvements to Addis. He angered the Eritreans by making Eritrea an Ethiopian province, taking away their sovereignty.

Eventually, dissatisfaction and a widespread famine led to the downfall of Emperor Selassie. Different factions fought to control the government. The conflict provided the opportunity for a Marxist movement to mobilize within the country, supported by the USSR. The intelligentsia of Ethiopia had plans for a parliamentary democracy but the military group who led the revolution, beginning in 1974, had other ideas. Selassie was formally deposed and a group of soldiers called the Derg took power. Many members of the former government were assassinated and Emperor Selassie died. The ensuing nationalization of private and church property created disorganization and uprisings. The Somali neighbors of Ethiopia took advantage of the situation by invading in 1978. If you wondered why a portrait of Che Guevara would be hanging in Ethiopia, it was through the efforts of the USSR and Cuban military units that the regime was able to beat back the advance. Further insurrections involving Eritrea and the famines that again ravaged the country led to the downfall of Mengistu Haile Mariam and his Socialist regime in 1989, but the ugly concrete structures with the hammer and sickle remain.

The succession of Ethiopian governments made a bad situation worse for the Eritreans, who continued to resist the loss of their identity. The resistance resulted in thirty years of war between Eritrea and Ethiopia, until Eritrean independence was finally recognized in 1993. The long war impoverished the Ethiopian treasury and left the border lands riddled with land mines, and the government was not able to provide for the soldiers when they came home. Hence, they now have beggars in the streets, a sad legacy for the proud Abyssinians.

Nutrition

On the morning of May 28, I walked to the office of MSF France in Addis Ababa. The gardens were beautiful and full of plants I knew well from Florida: lantana, hibiscus, oleander and bottlebrush, but there were also plants that grow in cooler climates such as hollyhocks and exquisite roses. With such a fertile, moist climate as exists around Addis it would appear that enough food could be grown to feed the country; but the infrastructure is lacking. I shared lunch with the native staff working at the office. There were the expected secretaries as well as the men who stock the warehouse and disperse supplies. These people were mostly of the Amhar tribe, the prevalent tribe in Addis, Their language is Amharic but they all spoke English. The staple was *injera*, a brown, flat type of pancake made of a native grain called *teff*. It is such an important part of the cuisine that they have woven tables shaped like inverted mushrooms to store it. Several different dishes; spicy lentils, a sauce heavy with curry, potatoes and carrots cooked together and stuffed peppers accompanied the injera. To proceed with the meal, two rolls of injera are needed. The filling is ladled onto one open piece of injera and pieces are torn from the second to soak up the sauce from the first. The men laughed as I watched to see how they would handle the piece of injera left on their plate. They simply rolled it up and ate it like a cannoli. There was no meat, but the grain must have enough protein because the Amhars are a stocky people, handsome and cheerful. The cost of the lunch was five *birr*, about 75 cents.

I was later to compare the Amhar diet with that of the Afar tribe. Though the goat's milk in the Afar diet as consumed in mission and the injera of the Amhars have about the same amount of protein, with two servings daily supplying about 16 grams, the Amhars eat lentils or other legumes with their injera. Two servings of lentils add another 12–18 grams of protein daily and there were other beans used in the sauces. Since the USDA publishes 56 grams as the minimum daily requirement for an adult man, that is well on the way to enough protein. Also, the teff with which the injera is made is relatively high in iron, each serving providing about 28% of the daily requirement. Milk has a negligible amount of iron. Though the Afar ate meat occasionally and the poorer Amhars not at all or infrequently, the Amhars did not appear to suffer the anemia that I would find to be common among the Afar. The vegetarian diet was easier to maintain on a daily basis. For these people, it's difficult to get enough calories. By contrast, with our meat-heavy diet in the US, we fail to appreciate that it takes eight times the energy (mainly in the form of grain) to produce a pound of meat as to produce one pound of vegetable protein. Using vegetables cooked in various ways and with different sauces is obviously the most satisfying and economical way to feed people.

In fact, according to the article, "Malnutrition is Cheating Its Survivors and Africa's Future," by Michael Wines in the *New York Times* (Dec. 28, 2006),[1] almost half of Ethiopia's children are malnourished. Most of the hungry survive but with stunted growth and mental slowness caused by insufficient protein in the first years. They also lack iodine and essential vitamins. As of 2006, flour and grains were not fortified in Ethiopia and salt was not iodized despite the fact that goiter is endemic in Amhara province. At the time of Mr. Wines' article, the Ethiopian government and UNICEF were caring for 20,000 malnourished

---

1 *World Hunger, The Reference Shelf* vol. 79 Number 5. Claire Stanford, ed. The H. W. Norton Co., 2007..

children. "[W]e can count 70,000," said the local nutrition expert for UNICEF—only "we can't treat them all." The men and women working for MSF were earning enough to feed their families adequately, one form of trickle-down economics that worked. At the MSF office, the gardens were kept by one old man who took great pride in his work. When I first saw the number of people in the compound in Addis, my efficiency index was alerted and I questioned the need for a gardener or for someone who makes tea and cooks, but after witnessing the industry of these people and the smooth flow of the work there, I came to realize that the mission of MSF is not just to save lives but also to improve them. It takes very little money to hire a gardener and the results are more than worth it.

A Gahla Welcome

Dominique, the Director of Missions for MSFF in Ethiopia, was an elegant Frenchman with impeccable English. He told me how eager they were to have a new Tech to send to Gahla. MSF had agreed to staff the hospital in Dubti with a rotating expat surgeon for training purposes but the hospital was still supposed to be responsible for drugs and supplies. Now the hospital had run out of TB drugs so the TB patients had been transferred to Gahla, but the doctors in Gahla, without a tech, were forced to send the sputum samples to the hospital in Dubti to have stains made and read. This had proved unsatisfactory as the sputum dried up in the climate and the results were unreliable.

At the guest house, Joel, the doctor who had been staffing the Dubti hospital, was preparing to leave and our housekeeper, Terafou, wanted to do the Coffee Ceremony for the two of us, a custom comparable to the Japanese Tea Ceremony. Terafou was of the Oromo tribe from the south of Ethiopia but the coffee ceremony is nationwide. For the ceremony, she brought in fresh grass to spread on the tile floor. She lit a brazier and patiently roasted green coffee beans. When they were brown, she ground them in a mortar and pestle, and then used a tall slender earthen pot to steep the coffee on the brazier. Coffee in Ethiopia is served in small glasses, black, with sugar. The Ethiopians were the first people to use coffee, reportedly after seeing how frisky their animals became after chewing on the leaves of the bush. With centuries of practice, they have perfected the art. It is smooth, not acidic. Terafou gave us the traditional accompaniment, popcorn.

Then it was time to inspect the laboratory kit destined for my lab. The kits devised by the planners at MSF are ingenious. There are surgery kits, OB kits, nutrition kits, lab kits and others. In any emergency the appropriate kits are pulled and shipped with no time wasted. This explains how MSF was able to have an inflatable surgery theatre and supplies packed and ready to arrive on the ground within three days of the earthquake in Haiti. My lab kit had a scale for weighing the components of our stain, White Blood Cell Pipettes for manual counts, a counting chamber, a clever devise for measuring hemoglobin, various reagents, two microscopes, filter paper and funnels, a hand cranked centrifuge, slides and slide cases and more. After I had verified that all components were in place, a driver took me to see the cabinets that had been chosen for our lab. They were made of heavy plastic and looked to be appropriate for the purpose. So far, so good.

Since the trip from Addis to Gahla took ten hours, the usual procedure was to do a "halfway." We began the journey in a car with an Addis driver. Halfway, we stopped at a truck stop, a building with a wide cement floored veranda on which tables were arranged. There were trucks, tankers and various conveyances parked around outside. There we met with Ali, a driver from our mission at Gahla. He spoke English and ordered an omelet for me. The chickens had obviously been able to forage amongst grass as the yolks were very yellow.

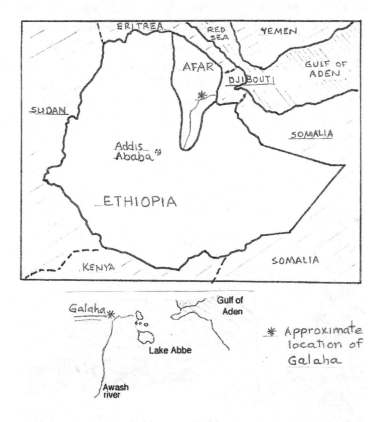

From there on we rode with Ali, an Italian-American doctor bound for the hospital at Dubti, and me all crammed into the cab of a Toyota pickup. The land up to that point had been rolling highlands.

The land was becoming drier as we moved east. We had no air conditioning. The heat increased and more dust came through the open windows. Close to mission we saw a flock of ostrich, the largest living bird. The black males are eight feet tall and impressive but the doctor was not amused; every twenty minutes he would exclaim about the increasing barrenness of the landscape. In fact, he only lasted six days and fled back to the comforts of air conditioned hospitals.

Trees became fewer as we rode along. Forests in Ethiopia have been reduced from covering 40% of the a country a century ago to only 3% today, according to a paper by Badege Bishaw, Ph.D, presented at the International Conference on Contemporary Development Issues in 2001. Many forests have been cleared to make the land available for farming but many trees go for fuel, in the city as well as in the countryside. Propane is expensive. Unfortunately, with sloping land such as this was, the lack of trees was contributing to erosion and loss of fertile topsoil.

The ride was rough and when we arrived in Gahla in the late afternoon it was hard to believe that the day had actually cooled off — the heat was like a blast furnace. The ground was mostly bare and unlike some deserts which are colorful, Gahla was dun. The Rift Valley, so named because it sits upon a volcanic rift, was once verdantly green but a collapse occurred when the Arabian Peninsula, originally a part of Africa, split from the main continent. The valley has sunk and widened over time until parts of it are more than 300 ft. below sea level. At this point, there was just a layer of pulverized volcanic rock between our feet at Gahla and the thermal activity beneath. In the distance, the highlands that we had left behind were still visible as purple foothills and toward the river I could see a strip of green and some stunted aca-cia trees, but the mission itself was all brownish-gray. The soil was a fine dust with less substance than sand. It was unadorned by grass. Only rocks broke the surface. In a small area enclosed by hand woven fences, there were a few small tents for us, the staff, an office on stilts built of unpainted plywood and a combination cookshack/dining area. Beyond the homemade fence there were two large hospital tents for the patients, various storage buildings, a patient kitchen and, up a rise, the laboratory. It was the only real building in the compound, built of ce-ment block hauled all the way from Addis but still unfinished because without a tech, there had been no reason to hurry.

Now I was that tech, and I was struck with a sudden dose of humil-ity. It was brought home to me in pitiless clarity that I was the only one responsible for setting up the lab, for turning out the results and for training native staff.

It is customary, due to the heat, for the Afar to begin work very early, to break between 11 AM and 4PM and to then work until 6 PM or so in the evening. Maria, the Greek nurse who served as head of mission at Gahla, took time to meet me. I was shown to my tent, an oven at that hour, and given a brief tour including the combination latrine and shower "building" where you could dump a bucket of water over your head.

We then walked down to the hospital tents. Patients were lying on the ground with only woven mats for beds but with IVs running and a standard medical care system seemed to be in place.

Vinod, an Australian doctor of Indian descent, was seeing patients in the "clinic," an anteroom of the tent where patients were weighed and meds dispensed. There were native people working in the hospital, young men who were part of APDA, Afar Pastoralist Development Association, who had received basic health care education as well as two professional native nurses, Afars named Hassan and Kadir. I met the logisticians, Fred, a Frenchman and Jose, originally from Portugal but naturalized French.

Lastly, I met Milton, the French-Canadian who founded this mission. Milton was a complex personality with rather grandiose expectations for his project. He told me how easy it was going to be to make this a permanent laboratory with trained staff from the Afar tribe, with expat personnel coming regularly to check up on their work (bear in mind how long it had taken to get the first tech).

Your Mission Should you Choose to Accept It

The first night was less than restful. My small tent with its one tiny window was indeed hot but more disturbing to sleep was that the hospital tents were just on the other side of a rudimentary fence from my tent. Not only did I hear the TB patients coughing but the mission was having a siege of whooping cough at the time and the kids cough until they vomit. Indeed, it is supportive treatment that they need to keep them hydrated until the infection finally passes. Added to this noise, I heard the hyenas.

The big push the next day was to get the lab finished. Jose was in charge of the operation and had been waiting on mastique (putty) to install the windows. Since we desperately needed to start staining and reading slides, considering the backup of patients, it was decided to stick the windows in temporarily without putty. When the boxes were opened, we found the putty was inside. Though I was eager to get started on "my" lab, there wasn't much I could do at that point. I tagged along behind Vinod as he did his rounds, getting a feel for the routine and meeting patients.

The Afar are an old people, nomads who have followed their goats and camels for centuries to Djibouti to the east and back into Ethiopia without concern for national boundaries. If the Afar speak any language besides Afaraf, it is likely to be French since Djibouti is French-speaking. They have been known in the past as the Danakil, the Dreaded Danakil, a fierce and warlike people. An old Djibouti proverb supposedly says, "Even a jackal makes his will before he crosses the Danakil." And indeed, though I had read about the practice, it gave me pause the first time my lab trainee smiled. His teeth had been filed into points.

The river had decided the location of this mission. Previously, MSF had tried to treat TB in the hospital setting in Dubti. The Afar people, however, depending on their herds as they do, would not stay put near the hospital in town, and they were defaulting on their treatment. This was a serious problem as we did not want to allow MDR (multi-drug resistant) TB to develop in a population which so far had avoided it. MSF was using a combination of ethambutol, isoniazid, rifampicin and pyrazinamide for the first two months of treatment in the hospital followed by rifampicin and isoniazid for the next four months on an outpatient basis. MDR TB develops when the infecting organism is allowed a reprieve during treatment with these first order drugs. This can happen when the patient wanders off before finishing his course of therapy and does not return on time. The remaining organisms may have developed resistance to the drugs when the same medications are started again and the patient can pass on the resistant germs to others. Today, with rapid air transport, an infected individual can carry the germ anywhere in the world so it behooves us to catch and treat the disease when it first develops. MDR TB is much more costly to treat because the second line drugs are more expensive.

MSF has long dealt with the problem of obtaining newer and more effective drugs for a developing world that cannot pay for them at Western prices. Ten years ago the situation had become acute. MSF was lobbying US and European drug manufacturers for discounts. MDRTB requires that the patient take up to 25 pills every day and, in some cases, an injectable as well. It was imperative that MSF get the best price. Since then, they have been able to purchase the second line drugs through a consortium called The Greenlight Committee. WHO

(World Health Organization) is a member as is MSF and others. The committee has been able to negotiate lower prices from drug manufacturers, but producing these second line drugs is not always profitable to the manufacturer. Though the incidence of MDRTB is increasing, the worldwide market is still small in comparison to, for example, a new drug to lower blood pressure or cholesterol, so only a few, or sometimes only one, pharmaceutical company will produce them. This scarcity of product increases the price. MSF estimates that the cost of MDRTB drugs for one patient under the Greenlight program is between $100-800, depending on how well the patient responds to the drugs and how long the treatment must last. MDRTB treatment can last two years. Even with this cost saving, the MSF website, after quoting the numbers, states, "These prices are far out of range of most health services in the developing world."

To avoid the occurrence of MDRTB, Milton decided to found a mission where the Afar could keep their herds and be close to their families, hoping this arrangement would help with compliance to the treatment regimen. Vigilance and proper record keeping would be easier, too, in a closed community. If a patient did not come for meds, we could search for him. One old man had disappeared from the program in Dubti, having decided to stop his pills for religious fast. Since he had returned to his kebele (village), he could not be found right away. Now he had reappeared at Gahla, requesting treatment. It remained to be seen whether he would respond to the first line drugs again.

Uncomplicated TB treatment takes a total of about six months with the last four months requiring the patient to come to the DOT's (Directly Observed Treatment) tent every morning for supervised administration of the meds. This may sound excessive but I heard numerous stories about patients who were given drugs in outpatient settings along with detailed instructions about how to take them, only to have the patient swallow the entire stock of drugs on the first day. Deaths had resulted from these misunderstandings.

I had a kerosene powered refrigerator in my lab with a thermometer. At six AM it read 38C, which is roughly 100F. That was long before the sun reached its zenith. I was told that it was routinely 120F every day. After the first day, I believed it. By 6PM I was sapped.

We again ate dinner sitting on mats under the stars. We had an Afar cook who had previously worked for an Italian family. He served spaghetti. Even without meat or cheese, it was good, but I didn't know then that he planned to serve it every night for the rest of mission. I had been told by the staff in Paris that my team would sustain me. I immediately felt comfortable with Maria who, despite being only 26, had already been on five other missions. She was Greek but her English was excellent and she also got by in French. Vinod and I formed a bond as the only native English speakers. He was a fine young doctor, only 27 years old, and it was his first mission, too. Fred had spent two years in the States and not only spoke English fluently but knew all of our idioms. He had been a sailor and pointed out the constellations. The sky was massive with no light pollution. Jose, the other log, had been on missions not only with MSF but also with Pharmacists without Borders. Then there was Milton. There was never any doubt about who was at the head of our non-physical table. Indeed, when I saw him striding across the desert with his retinue of patients and assistants, he certainly gave the impression of a messiah. In many ways, he had been one for the Afar people. There was a building very near mission that was reportedly a government health care clinic. However, there was no one in it and no indication that anyone ever had been. This mission, though we focused on TB, was already seeing everything. People brought their ailing relatives on stretchers, sometimes walking all night. Milton was the driving force behind the formation of Gahla and deserved credit for such an endeavor but I could already see that he preferred to second guess diagnoses and treatments.

The cook had two girls helping in the kitchen. They also did the laundry for the staff, laboriously using a scrub board and wash tub. Their names were Aisha and Saida. Maria had told them I was a grandmother and now the girls even refused to let me carry my bucket of water when I went to the shower hut. They took it from my hand and carried it for me.

In the evening the team shared histories and marveled at the new conditions we were seeing. Vinod had already found that most of the kids in mission had perforated eardrums from untreated ear infections. Maria told of the anemia and the need for protein in the Afar diet beyond that in milk. We all realized the connection between poor nutrition and lack of resistance to disease, particularly TB.

I had already seen my first two cases of Pott's disease, TB of the spine. One was an old man and the other was Mariam, a young girl only ten years old, both with the telltale humps on their backs caused by the infiltration of the vertebrae by the TB bacillus. In Pott's disease, paraplegia can develop due to the pinching of the spinal cord. Though Potts is the old name given to TB of the spine, TB can also attack other joints, most frequently the hips, knees, wrists and ankle. We all think of TB in the lungs, but it is a multi-talented and can attack several body systems. About 15% of TB is extra pulmonary, meaning outside the lungs.

If the TB germ is swallowed, whether in the patient's own infected respiratory secretions or in another form, stomach acid cannot be depended upon to kill the TB germ, Mycobacteria tuberculosis, or some of the other Mycobacterium species. Before pasteurization, Mycobacterium bovus from infected cows' milk caused infection of the tonsils and lymph nodes as well as the joints in the US as in the developing world. If the organism gets past the stomach, it can infect the bladder and kidney. We had a little girl in mission suffering with TB of the kidney. There was no time to lose in treating these patients as it has been estimated that one-half of patients with untreated TB will die within five years and that is without the additional problems of malnutrition and AIDS. In addition, each case of untreated pulmonary tuberculosis can spread the bacteria to 10–15 other people within a year. Though there are other routes of transmission, most often TB begins after being inhaled, hence the big push for sputum microscopy. Once diagnosis was made, treatment would be the same for both pulmonary and extra pulmonary TB.

Milton said that the patients and their families complied well with treatment in Gahla. They knew TB kills and they knew they needed medical care. As long as they could remain with their extended families and the livestock on which they depended, he felt that we could greatly decrease the incidence of infection.

June 5, 2001, was a red letter day in Gahla. Although we had the river very near, the river was low as well as suspect for contamination and the staff had been hauling water from distant sources. The water was carried in large canvas bladders by truck, the bladders being then stored under the office. Distribution of the water was a daily chore. Though we had encouraged the residents of our camp to use the water we provided since both animals and people defecated near the river, as the camp had grown, our supply had been taxed. But that day, l'Action contre la Faim, the French contingent of the NGO Action against Hunger, dug a well for us, going to 300 meters to get good water. When they hooked up the pump, the water gushed out very warm, a result of the thermal activity beneath.

Keeping the inside of the body hydrated was even more important. One of my first introductions was to my "gourd." The name remains from when the Afar used gourds for canteens, though we now used recycled plastic oil cans which were wrapped in burlap. If the burlap is dipped into water the liquid inside is cooled. All the "gourds" had a string for slinging over the shoulder and within a couple of days of arriving at mission, my gourd had become my best friend.

There was another reason for avoiding the river. It was a reservoir for Schistosomiasis, a parasitic disease picked up from bathing in infected water. It was OK to wade in the river while it was low but I had a hard time forgetting those Parasitology reference books. The larvae of Shistosoma hematobium find their way up the urethra and lodge there, blocking the passage of urine and causing serious bleeding.

Lab Report

Work was well under way in the lab. A large tank had been installed, at some peril to the worker, I think, because both the ladder he used to get up there and the frame for the tank had been made of saplings cut down by the river with the smaller branches for crosspieces. This was very clever of them, because by elevating the tank, I would have running water in the lab, the only running water in mission.

The lab had been built to WHO specifications, that is, with an anteroom where the slides would be made from the sputa with the door to the main lab closed. Masks had been provided in the kit. When the slides had been made and stained, the sputa would be capped and the staining area swabbed with bleach before the door was opened to avoid contaminating the main room with bacteria. The main room had counters installed on two sides and I was to use the sun as my light source for the microscope. One problem we had right away was the flies. Anywhere there is livestock there will be flies. In Gahla, they were everywhere, all over the goats and camels, all over the babies, and, though our food was served with covers over it, the instant we removed the covers, the flies found it. I was determined not to have flies in my lab, carrying bacteria on their feet, into an area that I needed to keep clean. I had plans and was eager to get started.

Milton told me there were far more birds at the river, so I walked the quarter mile that evening. Indeed, snatching insects out of the air were Carmine Bee-eaters. Carmine well describes the body color. The birds were nesting in the banks of the river, hundreds of them, popping into the holes they had excavated. I saw the four species of kingfisher that I would see in Gahla. The Malachite Kingfisher, had a turquoise head and bright red bill while the Grey-headed appeared plain but the blue of his wings was electric. In the African Pygmy Kingfisher, named for its diminutive four inch size, the sun's rays illuminated the face at the right angle to show me the glistening lilac and the Pied Kingfisher, "just" black and white, is adorned in an arrangement of stripes, flecks and the highest kingfisher crest.

I saw my first Salt's Dikdik that evening, a tiny antelope just fifteen inches high with back legs longer than the front ones giving it the appearance of a large rabbit. It was not yet rainy season so the water level was low with sandbars available to the birds in the middle of the river. On these sandbars were Thick Knees, both the Spotted and the Water Thick Knee. Common on the banks of the river were Helmeted Guineafowl. I had seen Guineas in the US but these were unique, with a dot matrix pattern of black spots arranged in curving swirls, bright blue face patches and a scaly horn called a Casque sticking out of the tops of their heads. Living and working in trying conditions, I needed these distractions. It was my team and the river that sustained me.

Chapter 2. Laying Foundations for a Functioning Laboratory

I am not by nature a patient person and clinical laboratory work requires a certain amount of efficiency. Yet there were no clocks in mission, and although I had my watch, I soon learned not to bother to look at it.

Potential TB patients were piling up waiting for their sputa to be tested, and Jose felt the stress as he was responsible for getting the lab finished as well as myriad other duties. MSF had hired a large number of native people to work on building the lab, storage sheds, future living quarters for the staff and also, as more and more patients came, deboiters (Afar houses) for the people to live in. These houses are just domed shelters formed by bending over pliant poles and covering them with the Afar mats. Afar women built the deboiters. There was a very traditional division of labor. The hired men were mostly assigned to the construction of the compound buildings and hospital tents. But, since most of them were not accustomed to construction work, they did not know how to proceed on their own and Jose was required to oversee everything. Right now he was supervising the final work on the lab.

Some of the windows in the lab didn't fit and had to be covered with tarps. The men were trying to tape the tarps up with cellophane packing tape. I did find one roll of duct tape in the office and brought it with some scissors to the worker doing the taping. I then learned my first Afaraf word, (spelled phonetically) Gott-a-gee, for thank you.

I had been concerned that I would not wake early enough to start in the lab at 6AM. That was not a problem. Prayers began for the Muslims at 4AM. Milton had decided that a great gift to the Afar would be a megaphone. Now everyone got called to prayer at that hour, including the expat staff.

I couldn't start staining samples because the sink was being tiled. I weighed out the reagents for the stains, mixed them and filtered aliquots for ready use. I put away supplies, stacking stains, slides and utensils in the new cabinets and cleaned as much as possible (after supplying the lab with bleach). Bleach is a necessity to kill stray bacteria and viruses. If the lab is not kept clean, surfaces, slides and microscopes can be contaminated with the TB bacillus. Not only is this dangerous for the staff but these stray bacteria can show up in the stained smear of a negative patient and result in a false positive.

It is unheard of in the US to treat patients on the basis of smear results alone as we have the luxury of cultures, fluorescent stains and PCR to identify the species of Mycobacteria, but smears were what we had in Gahla and I wanted them to be of the best quality.

Most US hospitals use a cold stain but we were using the old but very dependable Ziehl-Neelsen method which requires heating to set the stain. Mycobacteria tuberculosis is a very tough organism which cannot be discriminated with ordinary stains. Finding it requires three reagents. A magenta colored stain, called fuchsin, will color the bacteria in the specimen. Then an acidic decolorizer is used to leach the color from other bacteria while the TB bacillus retains its color. That is why it is called an AFB, Acid Fast Bacillus. The smear is then counterstained with a blue reagent so that the magenta colored TB bacteria will show up against a blue background.

It sounds easy but I ran into trouble right away. The windows were in but without screens, and I didn't want to open them to the flies. The lab was so hot by midmorning that I felt my head would burst. In the method we were using the red stain must be heated while on the smear to set it. Our commendable kit had included staining racks to lay across the sink and we used flaming bits of cotton batting dipped in alcohol (also supplied) to pass the flame under the slide. The smears are supposed to steam. Instead, the stain boiled immediately and left precipitated stain crystals on the slide. They looked messy under the scope and it made the slides hard to read.

The decision on whether to treat or not to treat depended to a great extent on these slides. The process began with the collection of three early morning sputa from each patient. If two out of the three samples were positive for TB bacilli, the patient would be treated. We did not want to miss positive patients due to unreadable smears. In the heat, the stain was already too near the boiling point before the flame was applied. I had to find a way to keep the stain liquid and even long enough for it to penetrate the bacteria. I left the lab demoralized. My mind dwelt with the problem as I washed my hands and went to breakfast.

I thought about the stain and how it could be handled. I often felt, during my time in mission, that I was lucky to be as old as I was. Maybe I didn't have the physical stamina of the young but I did have experience. When I began training in 1968, we did not have the autoanalysers seen in US labs today. I learned manual methods, very handy in the present situation. My kit had been supplied with filter paper to filter the stain when taking an aliquot from the big bottle because residue can form in the bottle that needs to be removed by filtration before the stain is used. At the hospital where I had been working in Florida, we used a cold stain for TB smears but we cut small pieces of filter paper to fit each slide before we applied the stain. We felt it helped to even out the color. When I went back to the lab I cut some filter paper to fit the dimensions of a slide and proceeded with a few more smears, making a thin prep from the sputum sample, letting it dry, laying the small paper on the smear and then applying the red stain onto the paper. I heated the stain very briefly, just until the first faint wisp of steam appeared, and then let the stain sit on the slide for a few minutes before continuing with the rest of the procedure. Macroscopically, the slides looked good. I was unable, however, to find out right away whether it would make a difference in the finished smear because the sun had moved.

We could only read smears from about 7:30AM until 9:30 AM and again from 2:30PM until 4:30PM. Those were the hours when the angle of the sun fell onto the mirror of the microscopes and directed the light in such a way as to illumine the smear on the microscope stage. And in order for the sun to be falling on the mirror, the reader had to be sitting in the sun. It was bad in the morning. When we moved the scope to the other side of the lab to catch the afternoon sun, it was murder. The immersion oil that is used on the slide to avoid diffraction thinned in the warmth and ran all over, greasing everything in the vicinity. Milton came up to the lab that day. He looked around and nodded approval of my arrangement of the lab equipment, then uttered what must be one of the understatements of all time, saying, "It is rather warm in here, isn't it?

The new smears were not dry. I explained that I was improving the process but he wanted to see the messy slides. I expected criticism but he was surprisingly patient, perhaps because he had had such a hard time getting a tech to come to Gahla. It was a wise course for him that day because I was too hot, too tired and too old to take any grief from him. I looked at the new slides later when the sun again made itself available and I had two plainly positive AFB smears to report. The slides had no residue and, in addition, used less stain and less alcohol with the modified method; one challenge down.

At first, there were always things to do during the break while the Afar rested and the sun hid itself from the scopes. We had a laptop computer in the office powered by a solar panel above the porch and an Excel program with which to make lab requisition/report forms. These forms would accompany the samples after being filled in with patient names and orders for the required test. I would note the results of my examination after reading the sputum smears and "quantitate" any positives on the forms as well as the results of my findings in any other lab test. It was a French keyboard with the letters in different places from our English pattern and with some unfamiliar characters. In addition, I had never used Excel, but Vinod patiently coached me. I remember thinking that, of all the things I had expected to do in Ethiopia, learning a new software program was the last one.

I readied slide boxes to keep the positive slides as required by MSF protocol. There were blanks to record the patient's name. We all struggled with the unfamiliar spelling, and since the Afar are often named after relatives, many of the names were the same, so we started to include the kebele (village) along with the names to keep the patients straight. Our system was coming together.

After we had decided as a team on the format for our requisition/report forms and I had done the layout on the computer, the gasoline generator was cranked up so we could print them out, fitting two requisitions on each sheet of paper to make it go as far as possible. Solar power would not generate enough oomph to run a printer. Generator use was always a team effort as the generator was much further back in the compound than was our office. We had no phones, of course, so someone in our office on stilts would run down and alert someone behind us in the medical tents. The second someone from the medical tents area would have to get a third someone, even further back in the compound, to crank up the generator. When the printing was finished, the same relay had to be done in reverse. We printed plenty of reqs at one time.

I had progressed in getting my stain correct and my boxes of positive slides labeled and organized by the time the Ethiopian Minister of Health showed up on an unexpected visit. His main interest was in the lab and I was able to show him a positive smear and explain the laboratory end of things.

No Free Lunch

Just a few days later, we had a strike in the patient kitchen. The practice had been to cook for the patients and for one person accompanying each patient. Now that our population had grown to two hundred people, it was impossible to tell who the designated caregiver was and whole families were showing up to be fed. Maria had been spending far too much of her time cajoling and exhorting the women in the kitchen who were doing the cooking. We had never intended to cook for that many people under the existing conditions, that is, on open fires in a dirt floored pole barn, three times a day. It was a massive undertaking.

The flashpoint came when it was decided to let a few of the recovering TB patients help in the kitchen. They had been through the initial treatment and were not contagious, but eight of the women kitchen workers suddenly quit, saying it was too much work and they were afraid of catching TB—as if they weren't exposed every day already.

When I first got to Gahla, I wondered why anyone got TB. In the developed world TB is associated with immune suppression and with cold environments, and as such could affect a worker in a meat packing plant. It seemed to me that, with the abundant sun, the bacillus would be killed; but I was not then familiar with the way entire families— grandparents, parents and kids, were all scrunched into one small deboiter, maybe twelve feet wide, with no windows. Add the habit of spitting on the ground at will and poor nutrition, and you have the makings of an epidemic.

Our native nurses were attempting to convince the kitchen workers that there was no danger of contagion, but the whole situation was out of hand. That noon, by necessity, most of the medical team as well as the kitchen help reserved for staff, spent a long time dishing up lunch. We served injera, rice and a goat stew. It was controlled chaos. It is the

Amhara who eat injera. The Afar professed not to like it. Yet not only were we feeding too many, some people were getting in line twice. The open cook fires were elevating the already miserable temperature and the cook shack had two corrugated metal walls that became hot to the touch. It was a real challenge to keep dirt out of the food when there was no place to set a plate down. Our staff, along with two women who remained steadfast at their posts, were obliged to maintain a bucket brigade of plates; kitchen worker dishing up one dish, cook dishing up another, lab aide passing to tech, tech to nurse, and nurse to diner—who then grumbled about the food. It was definitely not the best use of our talents. Maria became even more determined that something had to be done about the food situation.

The next morning the people got Plumpy Nut Bars, a nutritional supplement, for breakfast and we were told not to fix any lunch at all. Milton said this was necessary because the patients' families were supposed to be helping with their care, including cooking, but they had refused to do so after threats from the strikers who wanted less work for the same money. Who would have expected a picket line in the desert?

In the evening a group came representing the strikers and talked at length. A meeting was called for the next day to be held in the area on the outskirts of mission which was used as a mosque. That area was usually off limits to women but Milton marched Maria right into the midst of it and insisted that she be included in the negotiations. After some questioning back and forth between the leaders, she was allowed to speak. Maria explained that the plan was to procure foodstuffs and to then supply each family group with provisions that they could prepare themselves, resulting in far less work for the kitchen staff. The leaders realized that a move like that could eliminate jobs, and they backed down.

In camp that night, Milton advised us that we would have to hang tough with these people. He said he had been forced to leave Gahla at an earlier time because some militant Afar claimed they weren't being paid enough, though MSF already paid native labor more than did any other NGO. The situation was resolved and the women went back to work, but Maria said to me that evening that she was "determined to put an end to this endless cooking and get back to nursing where I belong."

On my way to the river that evening, several Afar people detained me. As a blonde, I had become accustomed to having the kids touch my hair and skin, but this time they wanted to see my bird book. They were very excited and started tossing out the Afar names for the birds they saw pictured. For the Spur-winged Plover picture, they called out, "Gaia." (I am giving it the phonetic spelling because the Afar language was only then in the process of being written down.) They were glad to have something to teach me and I was glad to see that they loved their birds. One thing to be said for the primitive lifestyle, human activities did not impact the wildlife. Many birds benefitted from the livestock as they fed on undigested grain in the droppings.

I saw the Gaia that evening surrounded with some small birds that turned out to be her young. The Black-headed Plover with its upswept crest and dramatic markings lived in Gahla as did the Namaqua Dove. Tiny male Namaqua Dove is memorable, with his black throat and napkin, strutting around with his bill in the air as if he was a peacock instead of a very small dove.

Vinod went to Addis during my second week in mission. I knew he needed it. When the team was left alone we operated smoothly but when Milton was around, we were no longer a team, just disciples. My opinion was always mixed regarding Milton. He did know the Afar people far better than we did and he proved to be correct in his handling of the kitchen strike. Maybe it was necessary to use a heavy hand with some of the patients and workmen, as he claimed, but there was no reason to use it on other members of the team.

Mohammed, one of the Afar foremen, took it upon himself to invite the Action Against Hunger staff to sleep in our compound and to eat with us while they were building the pump house. Milton exploded. I can't imagine why he would object to extending hospitality to a group who had made our lives so much easier. I think it was simply that he was not asked first. Maria told him that night that such behavior could not be tolerated. It was then that Milton told us that he would leave Gahla because, he said, "I can't change."

While Vinod was gone, I began to feel unwell. I had been experiencing "the runs" but didn't feel it was anything that needed treating. My thinking was that, in healthy adults, most diarrheas resolve themselves. This day, however, I crawled out of my tent in the morning and found that I weaved when I stood up. It was a peculiar feeling. I went to the hospital tents to get the sputa as I always did, but I must have looked peaked because Milton took one look and asked me if I was OK. I admitted to the distress and he advised me that "we can never ignore diarrhea in this climate. You will dehydrate far too fast." Milton was right. Despite taking the antibiotics he gave me, I don't think I ever completely regained my electrolyte balance after that day. The balance of sodium, potassium and chloride along with carbon dioxide are crucial for the human body to function properly and to facilitate the retention and expulsion of water from the tissues. I was losing too much water via perspiration while sitting in the sun at the scope, and losing it at the other end as well was making me sick.

Sign Language and Key Words

I had been assigned a lab helper from among the APDA young men who had been helping in the hospital tents. His name was Hammadou. Apparently, he spoke just two words of English, namely "Good Morning," but Hammadou was a quick study and it wasn't difficult to teach him to stain.

Laurence in Paris had advised me to draw the microscope field in color when I wanted to teach the trainee to recognize the TB organism in a smear. When I found a positive field, I had a blue pen and a pink pencil. I drew what I saw in the microscope field, blue cells and thin pink bacilli. There is a lot to see in a smear besides TB. There are white cells, cells from the lining of the respiratory tract, other normal bacteria. Some objects stained pink. Day after day, I drew the microscope field. Hammadou would stare at me blankly. It is not as easy as it sounds. Not only did he have to learn to use a microscope, including how to manipulate the coarse and fine focus and how to move the slide across the microscope stage: he also had to learn the shape and orientation of the slender pink rods amongst all the junk. As time went on, he began to look very crestfallen when he still didn't see the required object.

While we sat on the mats, I talked to my team about my inability to get my point across and asked for suggestions. They felt it would just take time. We were beginning to rely on each other, to expose our feelings. On the day of the summer solstice, the outside temp must have approached 130 degrees. The heat did not help my frustration but I stayed patient and continued making pictures. My satisfaction was mirrored by the others on the mat when, the next evening, I could finally report success. Hammadou, after another drawing session, looked back into the microscope, drew a sharp breath, held up his fingers very close together in a "tiny, tiny?" gesture and I knew he recognized the target at last. I then began to teach him to quantitate the amount of TB bacteria he saw in each slide as a correlation has been shown to exist between the increasing number of bacteria in the sputum and the potential of the patient to infect others. Quantifying was not nearly as difficult to teach. Thank God, despite the language difference, we both used Arabic numbers.

I was learning a few Afar words and could greet patients and residents with "Mahasennee," meaning Good Morning. I doubt if my pronunciation was accurate but they smiled and got the meaning. Goodbye or good night was Shalom. I did discover that Hammadou knew a few words beyond Good Morning the first time a slide accidentally slipped off the rack while he was staining. He knew exactly what to say as the slide dropped into the sink. That word, and "OK," seem to have become universal.

Beasts of Burden

I awoke one morning less rested than usual. Some of my neighbors had left a baby camel tied up near our tents and it bawled all night. We were frequently in contact with camels. I was frightened of them at first because it is only when you stand next to one that you realize how large they are. But the camels I knew were gentle beasts, or else they were just too tired and malnourished to give any trouble. What they ate is still a mystery. I did see them wrapping their prehensile lips around and among the wicked thorns on the acacia trees, the only thing around with any green, and that was minute. They had liquid dark eyes with extremely long lashes. I fancied the expression in them was resignation.

The Afar used their camels to travel from one camp to the next. When grazing was exhausted in a given area, the women (of course) would break down the deboiter, wrap the poles and roll up the mats which would then be attached to a sort of saddle. Onto this would be hung any cooking pots they had, clothing, jerry cans if they had them or the goatskin water carrier. If there was too much stuff for the camel, the woman carried it. Vinod came back to the dining room one day, irate about this custom. He had just released a young woman from hospital and her husband was loading her down like a pack horse for the trip home. Vinod complained so loudly that the husband did take part of the load but we both knew that, once the pair was out of sight, she probably got loaded down again.

Goats

Nothing was wasted at Gahla. Particularly impressive as a use of resources were the goatskin water carriers. They would skin a goat, sew up the slit in its skin, wrap the ankles and wrists tightly, leave a flap of skin over the neck hole and, voila, a water carrier, skin tight. The goats in mission were not large white goats but rather small goats, possibly Nubians, and one skin probably held close to two gallons. There was not a lot of trash in camp, either, as we were a long way from plastic grocery bags and superfluous packaging. One effort at recycling I had to quash. We did not immediately have a burning barrel for our sputa once smears were made. We were waiting to get a barrel from Addis. In the meantime, I took the sputa in their plastic cups up to the burn pit. It seemed the thing to do since the other trash should have helped them burn. I didn't reckon on the goats, however. A fence of woven twigs and branches had been built around the pit but one must never underestimate the ability of a goat to get into or out of an enclosure. Either the goats had gotten the caps off of some of the sputum containers or the caps had come off by themselves but I caught a goat licking up the sputum. Animals can get TB and can pass the TB germ in their milk. Goat milk is one of the main components in the Afar diet. We could not take a chance on this mode of transmission. Studies in Nigeria have shown that goats kept in close proximity to humans can even be infected with TB by contact with their tubercular owners. The udders of the goats could then be colonized by the bacteria and milk expressed from the animals could be swimming with the germs. We certainly didn't want to create a new reservoir for the bacteria in one species while we were trying to treat it in another. Hammadou was asked to dig a burn pit outside the lab building. We fenced the pit and we were managing to keep the goats out, but I came across a young Afar father one day pulling the cups out and inspecting them for usefulness. I didn't have the language to explain to him why it was dangerous to handle the cups but I think the horrified look on my face got the point across.

Luxury Items

Vinod returned from Addis with a welcome gift. I had brought leather sandals from home and the soles had worn out very quickly. He brought me new rubber flip-flops. They were the much preferred footwear in mission because the rubber sole protected the wearer from the burning sand. He also brought dates and oranges. The dates were by far the best I'd ever had. They were from Saudi Arabia, sweet but not crystalized. Small comforts were much appreciated as life continued to be hard.

The digestive problems persisted or new ones flared up. I lost my appetite. I could eat the breakfast and a small amount of the rice we had for lunch but I could hardly choke down three bites of dinner. Sometimes, when we obtained supplies, they would contain Navel Oranges grown between Addis and the lowlands. It was strange to see them in July when they are a winter fruit in Florida. Supplies were a problem. We got the same thing every time for supplies so we ate the same thing every time; bread for breakfast, rice with vegetables for lunch and spaghetti for dinner. I was tiring of it after two weeks but the rest of the team had been eating it for much longer. When they complained, the cook blamed Fred who was doing the ordering and Fred blamed the cook for not placing a different order. Nothing changed. Our Afar cook was very independent and left for time off whenever the notion struck him but the kitchen girls, Saida and Aisha, worked every day until 8PM, serving us three meals a day as well as doing our laundry, and doing it all with smiles. Most of the time we just ate what was cooked and shut up.

Children with TB

Early in June baby Oskar came in with his family. The Afar aides or interpreters were always with the doctors to interpret. They were told that the baby was eight months old. He looked more like eight weeks, with his stick legs and wizened old man appearance. His skin lay in folds and he also coughed. It was the first case I saw of Marasmus. Milton ordered sputa to be collected on the mother. The next day had the first positive smear and another the day after that. Both mother and child began treatment for TB, while two other children and the father lived in the compound. Maria is pictured with Oskar at intake. She felt that Oskar could catch up once the infection was under control and the mother was well enough to provide more milk. He would receive supplemental feeding in the meantime. MSF uses therapeutic milk, which must be given in small doses often, as many as eight to ten feedings per day along with porridge feeds and any local foods the child will eat. CMV, a complex of vitamins and minerals is also given along with rehydration

I

if needed. It was imperative that Oskar be suitably nourished as the brain will not develop normally without enough protein and the proper mix of essential fats, carbohydrates, vitamins and minerals during the first two years. Intervention after the first years will not entirely repair the damage to development.

TB is particularly hard to diagnose in children since they can't cough hard enough to bring up a proper specimen for microscopy. In the case of Oskar, we assumed that he was positive because the mother was positive, he was symptomatic and the disease could have been easily passed between mother and child. MSF has long hoped for a quick test that could be used in the field, however, particularly for children. Today, there is a manual kit test available to detect TB but, according to information in the Journal of Clinical Microbiology, June 2002, it has only a 39□50% predictive value so has not proved sufficiently predictive to warrant its widespread use. In the meantime, the decision to treat children is often made on the basis of symptoms alone since, with treatment, 80% of kids will recover from TB. Without treatment, at least half will die. Another problem in treating children with TB is the large number of pills that kids must take. Infected kids must take 9 pills every day. If they are HIV positive as well, they must take 16 pills. Another hope of MSF is for a combination drug as young children have difficulty swallowing all those pills.

Funding Better Solutions

The Global Fund, the world's primary funding mechanism for supporting treatment and prevention efforts against HIV, malaria and TB in the developing world, was undercut this year by major donors to $11.7 billion, slightly more than half of the target amount of $20 billion and less than the $13 billion needed just to continue existing programs. The US has decided to contribute $4 billion over the next three years, less than usual and other donors made cutbacks as well. In the meantime, considerable gaps are left in funding. The World Health Organization reports that another $37 billion needs to be spent on global health, every year, in order to meet the health related Millennium Development Goals. That estimate does not include money for research.

One of the newest funding ideas, proposed by MSF and reported on their website, has to do with a new Financial Transaction Tax which is being proposed by the European Union to be imposed on all EU-wide transactions. MSF is asking that a portion of the revenue from any such tax be devoted to global health. The idea of a Financial Transaction tax is not new. Already the international agency UNITAID finances programs through a tiny tax on airfares. Recently, a number of countries have proposed a "Global Solidarity Levy" on currency exchanges where all funds raised would go to fill the health and development gap. According to that group's estimate, a tax of only 0.005% on the four largest currencies could result in $33 billion a year. Money from such a tax would be hardly noticed by global investors but could go toward easing the shortfall of the Global Fund. Importantly, funds from a tax would be more dependable than relying on donations and the money would help to assure that patients would be treated before MDRTB could develop or spread, with money left over for treating or preventing malnutrition as well as the development of combination drugs.

In Gahla, to know that pills would be crushed for Oskar and a positive outcome expected was an affirmation that I needed when crossing the compound at 11AM. The sun was strong enough to heat my head through my straw hat, one with a fancy weave that my daughter had bought in the islands, fetching once, but sagging and worn after a few weeks in Gahla. It also exhibited loose straws and tears where the goats had gotten to it when I laid it down to watch birds.

Improving the Lab

On the plus side, screens had been installed in the lab windows. They were not screens with frames. Apparently such things were not available so the men had simply cut screen to fit and taped them in as best they could. It was enough. We could now leave the windows open without inviting the flies. If we were quick in going in and out of the lab we could beat the flies that were hanging around the door waiting for entry. When we were finished for the day, I covered the microscope and scale and closed the windows to keep out the dust.

When Vinod returned from Addis he brought a man who professed to have lab experience. He was Afar and his name was Reggae. He did not look well and I questioned the idea of having him work in the lab if his resistance was poor. Vinod admitted that he had been surprised to see how thin Reggae was when he began taking off his outer garments as they left the cool of Addis for the desert. He didn't have the symptoms of TB, however, and I did hope he could interpret for Hammadou, who I felt must have questions by this time, so he came up to the lab on his first day. Perhaps he did have some knowledge of making smears but Hammadou had already become more proficient in his ability to find the specific bacteria, showing the patience necessary to peruse one hundred fields on each of his share of the ten to fifteen slides we had every morning. Reggae had to sit down out of the sun and rest frequently and could not tolerate the hardship.

After I had read slides behind Hammadou for some time and assured myself that he was good, I began teaching him to weigh reagents and make solutions. It was amazing how much he could retain with very little language and no procedure manual. Though we didn't have the alphabet in common, he learned to use the triple beam balance with ease. He did write down numbers from the scale and he always got the measures right.

CHAPTER 3. TEAM LIFE: FLIES, HEAT, AND BACTERIA WITHOUT BORDERS

I have mentioned the flies but it is difficult to relate how much they impacted our lives. Still in my first month of mission, we began to see Trachoma. Trachoma is caused by bacteria, Chlamydia trachomatis, that flies carry on their legs. The flies love to get fluid from the eyes and they leave the bacteria in the process. The lashes become infected. They swell and begin to turn under. The continual rubbing of the rough lashes against the cornea of the eye results in blindness. Our staff treated the early cases with antibiotics and told the mothers to keep the flies off the children's faces but, with a growing population of both people and livestock, and inadequate sanitation, I don't know how much good it did. The national nurses constantly exhorted the patient families to use the latrine and avoid leaving feces around that drew flies. However, our one latrine was never meant for two hundred people and it soon became a mess. Jose had someone sloshing it with water daily but, as the day wore on, I dreaded to use it, which I had to do all too often.

We all had to take malaria preventative. Maria and I took Larium, generic name Mefloquine, a very effective drug that acts against P. falciparum, the most dangerous form of malaria. Maria told me that the men started out taking Larium also, but they were having nightmares and psychological symptoms, a well-known side effect, so they left off the Larium and switched to other drugs. Vinod told me he felt that, "If I had continued on the Larium, I would have gone mad." I told him, "If I go mad, it won't be the Larium. It will be the flies."

Aides, AIDS and Aid

Reggae became a patient instead of a helper within the first two weeks of his stay. With his symptoms of thrush, weight loss, etc., I suspected the worst as did the doctors. It was a concern to us that we could not test for HIV. He may have hoped to get better treatment with the Western medicine at our facility but I couldn't even keep HIV kits in the lab for diagnosis. The required storage temperature for the kits at that time was between 2 and 8C, and my fridge could not cool the interior to anything approaching that low level.

Symptomatically, we judged that the incidence in Gahla was low at that time. The majority of cases were in the cities, where the rate was much higher than the rate for Ethiopia as a whole, 6.4% of the adult population. But we all knew that the rate would go up. It was 15% in our next door nation of Kenya and a staggering 40% elsewhere in Africa, according to aidsinafrica.net. The men were known to visit prostitutes. They then returned to their wives, perhaps more than one wife. The infected women bore children who were also likely to become infected, especially since prenatal care was practically non-existent. HIV was bound to complicate TB treatment as resistance to any disease is compromised in victims of the virus and AIDS patients are subject to other mycobacterial species besides tuberculosis. We saw patients who had all the earmarks of the disease but without a definitive diagnosis, we could not treat for it

The National Institute of Health did a study as to why AIDS is spreading so rapidly in Africa. They ascertained that along with poverty, denial is a major problem. There is such a stigma against the disease that patients simply refuse to acknowledge their condition until it is too obvious to ignore. Another reason quoted is that women are economically reliant on men and so are obliged to tolerate behavior that is damaging to their own health. That explanation is certainly no surprise to me or to anyone else who has worked in a domestic abuse shelter.

My best advice to a young woman anywhere who wants to avoid a life of servitude and/or mistreatment is: Prince Charming is undependable. Master a skill with market value and be prepared to take care of yourself.

Programs with just that goal are being put into place in Africa. Kirsten Scharnberg wrote in the *Chicago Tribune* (Aug. 25, 2005)[2] about a group of women in Niger who took an initial loan from an international aid agency and turned it into a credit union. Now 84 female members own their own land. They are encouraged to grow crops on this land other than the millet which the people of Niger have eaten for generations but which contains so little protein that 262 out of every 1000 children in the region die before they are five. It is a difficult task to persuade them to grow peanuts and beans because the women are berated for not following tradition. They are able to buy the land only with the permission of their husbands and those husbands may then pressure them to grow millet.

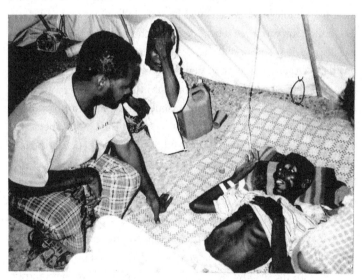

Another project, administered by UNICEF, buys goats for the women which multiply and provide not only protein for the family but can also be sold. Chetima Moustapha, an assistant project coordinator,

2 Reprinted in *World Hunger, op. cit.*

says that many aid agencies are focusing on the women because "there is a direct advantage to the children when women are helped. Women are always with the child, while sometimes the men go off to work in the cities."

As much as I admire the concept of these projects, I have to ask, if the men are going off to the cities to work, why is no money coming back to the wives and children? I very much fear that what comes back from the cities is AIDS instead.

Night Life

Unless visitors were present, Maria and I were the only non-Afar women in mission. We wore ankle-length dresses or slacks. We had not been instructed to do so but we had been advised not to insult the customs of the host country and the Afar women did not bare their legs. I did have a street-length dress that I wore to sleep in. Our tents, with their tiny windows retained the heat of the day, so they were almost unbearable for sleeping. I was hesitant to leave my tent and sleep out in the courtyard even when the rest of the people in our compound had already done so, but when I awoke one night with such horrendous hot flashes that I poured my "gourd" over my head in desperation, I gave in and dragged my mattress out into the common area with the rest of my team and the goats. I continued to use my tent for storing my belongings and I never had to worry about theft. My camera and binoculars were never locked away and no one ever touched them. I had a mat outside my tent to try to keep the dirt out, a hopeless task, but the mat served as a resting place for guests. When I returned from the lab in the evening I would go to my tent to brush my teeth which always felt gritty. Both Vinod and Maria visited separately, sitting on the mat, while I sat just within the opening, both areas shaded at that hour. They both recounted stories of love affairs ended just before mission. Perhaps the shadow made it easier for them to talk to someone old enough to be their mother. In turn, it comforted me to be a part of these young people's lives while I was absent from my own grown children eight time zones away.

What the Locals Do

The Afar "sheiks," religious leaders, administered their justice system. Addis and any form of national law were far away and never considered. When a rape occurred in the community during my stay, a council was formed and the victim's family received a large number of goats from the rapist's family. This may not seem a fitting justice to us but the system had the effect of encouraging families to keep their own members in line. If one member committed a crime, the whole family suffered by being fined. It seemed to work for them. Kadir, one of the national nurses and an Afar, was able to explain some of the Afar ways that I didn't understand. One custom that we all found abhorrent was female circumcision. Little girls routinely suffered infibulation, an extreme form of circumcision in which the clitoris as well as the outer and inner labia are cut away and the external vulva sewn together over the vagina, leaving only a small opening for urination or menstrual flow. And I don't mean this is done in sterile conditions. It is done by lay women with razors. When the girl marries the husband has to break through this stitching. I can only imagine what the wedding night is like for her. The stitching is perforce cut when she gives birth and then promptly is resewn, so that an Afar mother may have undergone the stitching and tearing several times, as many times as she has children. Milton had already had, as a patient, a little girl who could not urinate because she had been sewn too tight. Outspoken as he was, Milton railed to the parents about the practice and reported to us that the mother of the child had given birth to two more daughters and had not had either one circumcised. I applaud his insistence but I wonder what will happen to those girls. The circumcision is done to prove the girls are "pure" and to prevent infidelity. I hope the uncircumcised girls are not ostracized for their mother's good sense.

Kadir said that the national staff was trying to end the practice but he also said it was very hard to change something that had been practiced since the pharaohs. Indeed the practice is said to have begun in Egypt and female circumcision continues there today in some form as well as in other parts of Africa. I asked if it had to do with the Muslim faith and Kadir assured me that it did not. He said that today it is ostensibly based on a vague interpretation of the Koran but in fact it is an older tradition and not a tenet of the Muslim faith at all.

The Afar culture, probably like all cultures, was paradoxical. One day I was sitting beside Hammadou, both of us at our microscopes in the afternoon sun. I was parched, with sweat caking on my skin, when I suddenly felt a cool breeze. I looked up to see that Hammadou had removed his shirt and was fanning me with it. Despite the Afar culture's emphasis on being fierce, these people were also capable of tenderness and concern.

Expanding Our Scope

During my third week at mission, I went down to the compound for lunch and saw Fred, our log, lying on the porch of the office wrapped in wool blankets, visibly quaking. Maria informed me that it was thought he had malaria. He had not been taking the preventative, believing that it wasn't necessary since the rainy season had not started and there were no mosquitoes in mission. He had not considered that he was going to riverside areas to get supplies, and evidently he was infected there. I pricked his finger and tried to use the Geimsa stain that is preferred for malaria. I couldn't get it to work. The pH of the water is important in the staining procedure and our water was extremely alkaline. I tried Wright stain to make the smears, the stain used to examine routine blood cell components, but was never able to see the parasites in his blood—though he was treated and recovered. I knew then that I had to perfect a way to stain for malaria as the rainy season was coming. His case also convinced all of us to be diligent in taking our meds. Seeing him shake while wrapped in blankets in the noon day sun was lesson enough for me.

An old man came in to the clinic with a large swollen lymph node. TB can be carried to the lymph nodes, particularly the ones in the neck, a condition called scrofula. Scrofula can also be caused by other forms of Mycobacteria besides Mycobacteria tuberculosis and it is the most common form of non-TB Mycobacterial infection in children. We knew that the most common way for TB to spread to other sites in the body is to colonize the lungs first but this man's sputum samples were negative. Milton still felt that the most likely culprit was Mycobacteria, given the prevalence in the population. He biopsied the node and I stained several sections but could not find any Acid Fast Bacilli in the smears. Milton was disappointed not to get a definitive diagnosis but lab techs have been disappointing doctors ever since the two have been working together by not reporting the test positive that would end the doctor's quest. It was finally decided to send the man to the hospital in Addis at MSF expense. He turned out to have a cancerous lymph node. Diagnosis wasn't easy with no CAT Scan, MRI or even a histology department with the appropriate stains.

The doctors were beginning to use our lab for other tests besides stains. I did a wet mount on a stool and saw the eggs of Ascaris (round worm) and many flagellates. On another stool sample, I attempted a modified acid fast stain for Cryptosporidia, a parasite that causes debilitating diarrhea and can be fatal, especially in AIDS patients. I tried twice but I never found it. Clinical laboratories in the US are heavily regulated and controls are required for almost any procedure. In the modern microbiology lab, we have control slides made from known positives, which we use to make sure our stains are performing properly. I never had doubts about my AFB or Wright stains in mission as positives were demonstrated regularly but I missed the comfort of a control slide when I was developing the Crypto stain. I did not have the wherewithal to make a concentrated preparation and it was impossible to be sure, without a known positive, whether the stain was not properly functioning or whether the stool was simply too dilute. I considered consulting Laurence via e-mail but fortunately, the treatments which our physicians used to treat the diarrhea were effective, so definitive diagnosis of those patients was not necessary.

Diarrheal illnesses kill about 2.2 million children each year, according to UNICEF. Yet, the treatment is simple and cheap. Supportive treatment, giving a glass of prepared rehydration fluid following each defecation can prevent 90% of deaths. A packet of rehydration salts, containing electrolytes and sugar, is said to cost only about 10 cents, prepackaged for mixing in a liter of water on the UNICEF website, or a substitute can be made at home with sugar and salt. If you do a search online using the keywords "rehydration salts," you will see the UNI-

CEF website; but you will also see the site for Amazon.com. Amazon offers rehydration salts, also in packets for one liter of water but they ask $11.95 for a box of three packets. This is just one small example of the disparity between American drug prices and what medicines can be sold for when made available in generic form.

I was sometimes called down to the hospital tents to do hemoglobins. We had a clever method involving a device with two small windows of glass fitted tightly together. The blood from a finger prick would run between the plates. It formed a thin film of a standard thickness. This patient film was on the left of the device while on the right was a wheel containing colored films of various concentrations of hemoglobin. I could hold the device up to the light like a View Master, spin the wheel and compare the color of the blood in my patient film against the color in the sample films and find a match. It was a shock at first to find that I had to start looking among the lower concentrates for everyone, even ostensibly healthy adult males. The Afar diet of goat milk and bread did not provide much iron and parasites didn't help. Normal hemoglobin levels in the US are 12□18 grams/deciliter of blood. I rarely saw anything above 9 grams and usually lower. Maria was diligently trying to improve the diet of the Afar but again, we were dealing with hundreds of years of custom.

At first, when I saw the low hemoglobins, I thought of Sickle Cell Anemia which is seen in American Blacks. Vinod told me that he had not seen any Sickle Cell Disease and, in all the smears I did for malaria, I never did see any of the trademark sickle shaped red blood cells that are suggestive for the disease. Sickle Cell Anemia is hereditary. People who carry only one defective gene, that is who are heterozygous for the disease, may be a little anemic and a few sickle cells may be found in their blood smears, but the normal hemoglobin gene allows them to function normally. We call having just one copy of the gene the Sickle Cell Trait. I never saw any indication of the trait in the patients of Gahla. This was a blessing as a child who inherits the defective gene from two carrier parents has full blown Sickle Cell Disease and suffers sudden episodes of ischemia caused by occlusion of blood vessels. The parents suffer having to see their child in terrible pain. Later, I researched the subject and found that the disease is mostly found in Middle and West

Africa. It has been known for some time that having just one copy of the Sickle gene confers some protection from malaria, at least from the complication of cerebral malaria. We certainly had the malaria but the absence of the gene in the Afar was a clear indication that these people originated from a different gene pool than did the majority of American Blacks.

The distance patients had to travel often negatively affected outcomes. We had a boy brought in that Milton had treated recently with Ampicillin for tooth abscess. Many of the Afar had very bad teeth, not surprising since all they had to use for tooth hygiene was a stick which they chewed to fray the ends and use as a toothbrush. Ampicillin is an amped up form of Penicillin, and Penicillin is still a wonder drug in areas where it has not been overused and fed to livestock. Ampicillin should have done the job, had the family brought the child sooner—or returned sooner so he could have had longer or more intensive therapy. But, by the time the child returned, his bladder was greatly distended. Milton did a suprapubic withdrawal of urine, meaning that he entered the bladder through the belly with a needle. When the pressure was released, the urine started running out normally but the child was lethargic and his eyes were not tracking. Milton did a spinal tap. Reagents for Gram stains were included in my kit and I was glad I had perfected the procedure in advance. Ordinarily, the CSF would be spun in a centrifuge to concentrate the organisms and make it likelier to find them but our hand cranked centrifuge was not up to the job. Centrifugation was not necessary as I was able to see Gram positive cocci in pairs and chains in the fluid without concentration, Streptococcus pneumoniae or, as the Afar called it, Pneumococc. In the MSF clinical guidelines, Neiserria meningitidis (Meningococ) is the number one cause of bacterial meningitis and I had been vaccinated for Meningococcal meningitis, but both cases of meningitis that I saw while at mission were due to Strep pneumo. Apparently, the bacteria in this child's spinal fluid came from the mouth but it was reasonable to assume that in many cases, the Pneumococ spread to the meninges from ear infections since Vinod had already discovered that otitis was common among the Afar. In the States, about 50% of bacterial ear infections are caused by Strep pneumo. This child lived, though he appeared to have brain damage.

The national staff assured us that the family would take care of him but what a difference early medical intervention could have made.

Toward the end of June it began to rain occasionally. The rainy season provides the life blood for the Afar as the Rift Valley receives less than seven inches of rainfall per year. Far more rain falls in the highlands around Addis and that rainfall feeds the Awash River. The banks flood and grass appears to feed their stock. The rain started during the night and I had to drag my heavy mattress back into the tent. It was good to have the dust settled but we all knew the mosquitoes would follow. We were also beginning to feel the effects of our way of life. I hurt in every joint and it became a trial to get up from the mats. Doing without chairs had taught me to squat and, due to years of Yoga practice, it had not been a hardship before. But little by little, I was losing flexibility. Vinod told me that many of the older Afar complained of joint pain and he believed it to be due to dehydration of the joint fluid. Milton noticed me rising with difficulty from filling my gourd and demonstrated kindness itself when he told me that I needed to go for rest in Addis more frequently than the every five weeks that we were scheduled to go. He said, "You know, you and I are not as young as the others." This from a man who was probably not much above forty, close to fifteen years younger than I. Milton could be undeniably charming.

Routine was well established in mission. Though most of the expats had given up wearing watches, we all seemed to dribble in for lunch at the appointed time. The Afar definitely knew when it was 11AM and time to break until 4PM. I found lunch to be tasty. Hamadini cooked rice and he did it well. He incorporated grated carrots and sometimes spinach and occasionally there was a side dish of small sliced tomatoes. Olive oil was available and lemons. I made sure I used the lemons both for taste and the vitamins. The only thing wrong with lunch is that he fixed the rice every day just as he fixed the pasta every night. I was very tired of the pasta and Jose was very tired of the rice, sometimes exploding in a torrent of French when he lifted the lid of the serving dish to display his nemesis once again.

Our interpreters, Hiyu and Ayub, usually joined us for lunch. Hiyu was very well informed about world affairs as well as medicine and was always good company. Ayub always reminded me of Sammy Davis Jr. with his lithe body and quick dark eyes. The dining area was just the extension of the kitchen with a mat hung between. The table wasn't one as Westerners would think of it. It was a homemade effort using a larger lower board which sat on the ground and another tier of a smaller board elevated in the middle. Both were covered in blue plastic tarp. Over time the diners had tried to make the room into a lounge by laying woven rugs on the ground. We sat around after the meal discussing plans for the settlement, cultural issues and the comings and goings of staff. Weaver birds, Vitelline Masked Weavers for one, had colonized the thatch above our heads and made much squeaking and chirping music to accompany the conversation as they passed in and out of their colony. I was concerned at first about Salmonella, which is normal flora in all bird droppings, and we were certainly within target range as we sat there with our food underneath them; but there were so many bigger things to worry about in Gahla, we all acquiesced to living in symbiosis with the birds. We provided the thatch and they provided vibrant life.

I had been in mission about six weeks and was overdue to go to Addis for rest and relaxation. This was a necessary break as we worked seven days a week. The Afar took Friday, the Muslim Sabbath, off, but we saw patients that day, too, and I did the smears by myself. There was too much work to take time off. For this reason, I did not want to go to Addis until I got my assistants to the point that they could be relied upon to read both TB and malaria smears. My second apprentice began on the first of July and teaching him was much easier because Hammadou stayed on for a time to interpret. The new boy's name was Adais; he was a cute kid with a ready smile and very eager to learn. We worked on staining blood smears and finally were able to get Wright stain to work for both thick and thin smears. We were as ready as we could be for malaria season.

One day an excited child came to the lab, weaving his hand in a horizontal sine wave pattern followed with a biting motion. It was a great way of telling me there was a snake. I went outside and there was a sand colored snake which I couldn't identify, but assumed that it must be important if he was coming to tell me. I got one of the national nurses, who told me it was a soft scaled adder and poisonous. Fred, who was a sensitive soul, did not want to kill it but Vinod felt that it could get under the patient's mats and cause harm, so it was dispatched.

Fred was a lovable guy, tall and skinny and ready for anything but paperwork. He was not a good fit for the payroll he was stuck doing, along with the ordering of supplies. There were many differences of opinion between him and Jose, who was much more experienced and overburdened with the job of not only seeing that deboiters were built fast enough to accommodate the burgeoning population but also, at the same time, with getting living quarters built for the staff. I had never thought of the French as having a "Latin" temperament but the gesturing and passion of the arguments between those two showed me otherwise. Tempers got short in the heat but Fred never stayed angry. He was an optimist who made the best of every day. He adopted the wearing of the kurta, the cloth that Afar men wore wrapped around their legs, though it wasn't made for people of his height and his long legs hung far below the hem. Fred visited the Afar in their homes. He struck up a friendship with an Afar woman named Zahra about this time, which worried the rest of the team as we did not know how the relationship would be accepted by the Afar culture. It was reported by some national staff that there was grumbling in the Afar settlement about Fred's association with Zahra. She was not a maiden, having been married off to her cousin in the Afar fashion, only to then refuse to sleep with him. Apparently no one was able to force her to do so and she remained aloof, with the reputation of being a little crazy. She had money of her own as she was being paid by MSF to help with building deboiters for patients, so she could afford to parade herself around, wearing a varied wardrobe and all her bangle jewelry, which was considerable. Not for Zahra the black veil. She was daring enough to wear a bright scarf wound around her head turban style or as a sweatband, not really attempting to cover her hair. Her carriage was upright and regal, leading Milton to call her the "High Fashion Model of the Desert." Zahra was certainly a character and fascinated Fred. Neither Maria nor I knew how close this friendship had become and, if the men knew, they weren't telling.

Over time, I noticed that almost all the women had jewelry and it was explained to me that they used their jewelry as a form of insurance. They collected as much as possible during the good times, such as while they were working for MSF, then sold it when the droughts came and they needed to buy food for their children. I hope the depreciation rate was not as high as it is on jewelry in the West.

Life in Mission

I can only imagine that the dust storms were a precursor of the rainy season. I had cleaned the office one day during our midday hiatus. We had a medical library of sorts and the books had become covered with dust as had the computer and tables. I felt the wind picking up so I moved the ostrich egg that we used to hold the door open, closed the door and started closing the wooden shutters to cover the windows of the office. The force of the wind grew stronger. I weighted the shutters with rocks to keep them closed and my clean surfaces intact. Maria came into the office and told me that the sky was very dark. She had no more than shut the door behind her when the wind struck. It came from the east. The storms always came from the east, bringing half the Arabian Desert with them. We sat on a wooden bench, back to back, while the room went dark and the whole office shook on its pilings. I know we could feel each other's fear as the wind howled and we could see nothing. Buckets, loose boards, pans left out for washing, clattered around the courtyard and the dust found its way around the shutters and covered everything in a white film. Then, as quickly as it began, it was over. We went outside to a mess. Our tents had blown down and mine was ripped. Clean laundry that had been hung over the fence was scatted in the dirt and there was clutter everywhere. The kitchen and dining area had been spared, however, and we waited there as the rest of the team began drifting in, much to our relief. Vinod's black hair was covered in white and everyone was gritty with the dust. My cleaning job had been ill timed, indeed.

Jose could now add the job of temporary housing to his list of to-do's. Maria told me that they were advised in Paris to work on living quarters first before trying to add patient facilities but Milton thought it was imperative to have the patients and families housed first. Maria said she now felt that Paris had been correct as we were all getting tired and there was no place to rest. The tents were too hot and the dining room was too small for everyone and no respite from the heat. Maria felt the needs of the team acutely. She felt herself, as head of mission, to be responsible for everyone's wellbeing. It was a tall order for a little woman of only twenty-six years but she was a whirlwind of industry. She oversaw the patient's kitchen, our kitchen, the supply of meds, the ordering of bed nets for patients and staff as well as nursing duties. Probably more challenging, she kept the peace among the men and smoothed relations between expats and the native staff. All this and she was beautiful, too, with long brown hair screwed up tightly in a bun all day but worn loose down her back in the evening, classic Grecian features and a fine intellect. She told me she had never learned to drive as, on her island, cars weren't necessary. She had wanted to become a doctor but in Greece the State pays for college if you have high enough test scores, and her scores were not high enough to earn her a place in medical school. We were very lucky to have her as our nurse.

Just before the fourth of July, I listened to the Voice of America on the radio with the Afar. I laughed to hear it prefaced with Yankee Doodle Dandy. Voice of America is broadcast in four Ethiopian languages and the men were very interested in the broadcast. Americans were welcomed in Ethiopia at that time and I was sometimes called "America" by the patients. I was the first American some of these people had ever seen.

Fred recovered from malaria but, in his zeal to fully immerse himself in the Afar culture, he picked up their bad habits, too. He began to chew *kaat* (which Europeans spell *khat*). Kaat is an evergreen shrub native to East Africa. It is classified as a Schedule I narcotic in the US and is illegal here as well as in Europe. According to the Partnership for a Drug Free America, it causes "manic behavior and grandiose delusions." I did not see such an extreme effect among the kaat chewers in Gahla. It did appear to have amphetamine qualities. Many Afar men chewed the leaves daily and many of their social gatherings revolved around it. It was important for the men to have *dagu*, which means news, and they could spend hours exchanging dagu. With the kaat, they became very loquacious and energetic but I observed that it was hard for them to harness this energy while under the influence. Though Fred complained about having too much to do, he didn't seem very organized in doing it. He was a fun person to be around, however, and I could forgive him his faults. It was his first mission and I don't think he was doing what he had in mind when he signed up.

One of the greatest pleasures I experienced in mission was the camaraderie we felt while sitting on the mats under the stars in the evenings. Dinner was served to us there. We had clever solar lights manufactured by BP. There was a solar panel on one side which stayed exposed to the sun all day. At night we simply flipped it over and two fluorescent bulbs gave plenty of light. After dinner we shut the lights off. We had no TV, just passing satellites overhead and each other. I learned to recognize Scorpio in the sky and Sagittarius. Vinod had brought some CDs from home, one of which was the sound track from "Oh, Brother, Where Art Thou?," bluegrass music I never expected to hear while sitting on the ground in the Rift Valley with the silhouettes of camels outlined in the distance.

Milton loved to tease me about George Bush while I staunchly defended myself as not having voted for him. I had never used the slogans personally that we see plastered on cars or buildings, "America's Number One" or even "God Bless America" but I'd also never given thought to how insulting those kind of sentiments can be to other countries.

Fred tactfully brought up the idea that Europe in general views the USA as an aggressor though he saw Americans differently, having lived for two years among them. All my team members including the Afar staff knew far more about my country that I did about theirs. Though I had tried to read in advance, I knew that I was woefully ignorant about the history and even the geography of Africa. I felt embarrassed when the interpreters could rattle off the politicians of the whole Middle East and Africa as well as those of the West but Milton said that it was the same in Canada. He felt that it was because our countries are so big. He said that we in the US are usually aware of what is going on in the other states as the Canadians are aware of the provinces but that the countries in Europe and Africa are smaller and more likely to directly interact. That may be true but we found out in the US not long after those conversations on the mats that what we don't know can hurt us.

We discussed patient conditions and bounced ideas off each other about diagnoses and treatment. I experienced the sense of being part of a team that I had been missing in my job at home. Vinod informed us that voting was mandated in Australia. They all talked about their various national health care systems and marveled that I had been forced to quit my job in order to take the time off to come to mission. I groaned when they talked about their month long vacation allowances and generous family leaves. Some marijuana was brought from Addis and they asked if I had any objection to the smoking of it. I assured them that I was a child of the sixties and certainly had no objection; but I declined to partake as my joint pain was worsening and I feared that I might be forced to go home early, where pre-employment drug screens awaited me. My team had never heard of pre-employment drug screens. We had real cultural interchange.

If I finished with my smears before clinic was over for the morning, I liked to go down to the hospital tents and learn about any new medical discoveries. One day Vinod showed me a case of Madura Foot which he said he had also seen in the warmer parts of Australia. It was a nasty infection that had spread from an original small wound to the foot, possibly from a thorn, to form adjoining infected cysts with scar tissue in and around them. This poor patient had been walking on the mass for years. Vinod had to do a debridement before starting the patient on drugs. Untreated Madura foot can kill and it is a slow, miserable way to go. Mission was a pathology textbook brought to life.

I had bought stamps in Addis but I could only send letters infrequently, when someone was going to a post office. I don't know if I could have stood the isolation of mission if it had not been for our satellite phone. Once a week we would power it up and our e-mails would come in while those we had prepared in advance would go out. Maria was very careful of the amount of time the phone was in use as it was expensive. Usually it was the next day before I could access my downloaded mail and read the messages from Merle, who had not disappeared after all but could be relied upon to send both e-mails and letters. There were brief notes from my daughter and son. I discouraged others from mailing as I did not want to take up the phone time. The phone was also my link to Laurence in Paris for lab questions. When I couldn't find tubing for my white cell pipettes, it was she who advised me to cut some from the IV tubing which fit perfectly.

I went to the river less often. When I had still hoped that my joint problems were due to the unaccustomed lack of chairs, I had made a cushion of sorts for the homemade stool in my lab. But it didn't help. It didn't seem to matter whether I sat, squatted or walked. I hurt all over. The river and the birds beckoned but the trip seemed too far.

In the first week of July, Milton left Gahla. He was truly a non-material person. He took his boom box and speakers but gave away almost every other possession he had accumulated. He gave me a fine Afar milk basket, a twenty inch tapered cylinder with pedestal bottom and a knobbed, tightly fitting lid. The basket is double woven so that it is water tight inside with a beautiful design worked into the outside layer. I could still faintly smell the milk that it once held. It had been given to him by the Vice-President of the Afar state and it sits today on exhibit in my living room, one of my most valued possessions. Milton was never meant to function as part of a team. He needed to be the one who went before, the one with the grand vision, while others filled in the details. He also had a great sense of humor and we laughed many times, one such time being when he asked me if I was picking up any French. I told him that I had learned three things; the first, "ça va?" I learned in Paris, which is used for greeting everyone, and the other two

I learned from him, number one being "comme ci, comme ça," which he used often with a hand rocking motion to tell someone it could go either way and lastly, the vehement, "AI YI YI YI YI!" he so often used with accompanying head pounding to express his intense frustration with all of us. He denied that the AI YI YI was French but laughed anyway. I followed his career with interest and I'm glad to know that he went on to other missions and accomplished other goals. Life was easier without him, but he was missed in Gahla. A character like Milton leaves a hole.

Momin, one of the Afar staff, whom Milton had dubbed the "only fat Afar," gave Milton an Afar jile, the scimitar-shaped knife peculiar to the tribe, and I asked him to get another one for me. I wished that I could go with Momin to buy it and see more of Ethiopia than our patch of desert scrub, but I was needed for diagnosis of patients. Sometimes it seemed that everyone else was going somewhere. Our cook, Hamadini, took off on another of his unauthorized leaves. The kitchen girls probably could have cooked the spaghetti by themselves, having done it under supervision at least fifty times, but Maria and I took the opportunity to cook something else. I had discovered a box of lasagna noodles brought by some member of our group when they first came to mission. There was a piece of meat in the freezer of the kerosene fridge in our dining hut. It was always a mystery to me how the refrigerator section of these appliances would barely cool but the freezers kept meat rock solid. This meat had been in there for a long time and the cook, despite the fact that we were starving for protein, would not cook it because it "might have come from a Christian butcher." In Addis all the butcher shops are marked with crosses or the crescent moon and God forbid that one should eat meat from the wrong one. Maria and I had no idea where the meat had come from and, at that point, we didn't care. It took me close to an hour to get the chunk of iced-in meat out of the freezer, with water warmed on the cookfire and careful prying. When it finally emerged from its icy cocoon, with a sigh of relief from me, Aisha and Saida thawed and cooked it, then cut it into small pieces. Maria took it upon herself to make a béchamel sauce. Unfortunately, we had only therapeutic milk which is sweetened and the only cheese we had was some smoked cheese from Addis that had been hanging around because no one liked it. We did have a small propane stove as well as the cookfire and we found a huge kettle that barely fit in the oven. We baked and served our creation in that kettle. It was lasagna such as we had never had before and shall never have again. The Afar staff didn't like it and said they went to bed hungry. Our expat staff was kind enough not to complain but Maria and I found it delicious and even ate the leftovers the next day.

The men missed meat. Jose asked one night, in his rudimentary English, "Maria, we could have, mebbe, meat?" We sometimes tortured ourselves with what we most wanted to eat. Vinod wanted seafood; Fred wanted ice cream. I wanted, of all things, cottage cheese. Maria, God love her, made the best of anything and never complained.

Chapter 4. It's the Simple Tools that Work

Hassan, our Afar nurse and a moving force amongst the patients, brought a tech from Addis who he hoped would be able to work in the lab. He was Afar and I didn't doubt his credentials, as he was an older gentleman and had worked in laboratories for a long time before retiring. He spoke French but, since I didn't, we had communication problems. He called the TB bacillus Beka, for Bacille-Koch, the organism's original name, after Robert Koch who discovered the bacilli in 1882. He did not do staining as apparently the professionally-trained staff in his labs had done only reading, not the manual tasks. He missed some organisms in the slide I gave him to read but I knew it took time to get used to the brightness of the field when sitting in our ultra-powerful sun and to make the adjustments. I hoped that he would work out, both because he could act as a relief tech for me and also because he was such a courtly gentleman, bowing slightly when we were introduced and giving me the Gallic "Enchanté."

Let There be Light

After about five weeks, a child was brought in at night after I had gone to bed. Vinod suspected cerebral malaria and needed a smear to confirm. Maria was apologetic when she woke me. I told her not to hesitate as none of us resented helping in an emergency. However, they had forgotten that without the sun, I couldn't do any microscopy. We could not ignore the fact that it might be meningitis rather than malaria, so Vinod did a spinal tap. I used a flashlight to stain blood films for malaria and to make and stain smears of the cerebrospinal fluid, then tried shining the flashlight on the microscope mirror as a last resort for reading. But the light was not sufficiently concentrated to illuminate the field. I could only leave the slides for morning. As soon as possible, I slid the first smear of the CSF under the scope and saw the purple pairs and chains of Pneumococcus just as I had with Milton's patient. With no way to pin down the diagnosis, Vinod had treated the child for both malaria and for bacterial infection so the child was saved, but the drugs he was given for malaria were wasted as the child did not have it and there is always a slight risk in giving any drug. I was frustrated with my inability to read the slide right away and provide instant information.

The sun remained a limiting as well as a punishing factor. We could not get all the smears made, stained, dried and read in the morning before we lost our sun, so we got them ready in the morning and screened any that we did not finish when the western sun came available. Jose had wired the office for lighting using solar power panels which also provided the power for our laptop computer. By this time we were able to communicate to some extent and I asked him whether he could set up solar panels for electricity to the microscopes so that we could use the bulbs for the microscopes which had been included in the kit. He had never done that before but he promised he would try.

True to his word, he arrived in the lab the next day and mounted a solar panel outside, then proceeded to wire not only the microscopes but also to put an overhead light in the lab itself so that I could work at night. We read smears that afternoon sitting at the counter out of the sun. It was none too soon. That morning, my bladder had felt heavy and sore. We could not drink enough to replace the water we were losing and sitting in the sun had not helped. That merciful effort by one wiry Portuguese-Frenchman made it possible for me to continue at mission.

The solar energy we used at mission was generated via solar panels about 33 by 21 inches. One panel ran the laptop and lights in the office and another easily ran the lights and the microscopes in the lab. Panels such as these are listed on the BP website as costing $295.41 to Americans. After having the utility of this readily available power source demonstrated to me, I now question why we, as a nation, continue to rely on oil for the vast majority of our energy needs.

During the second week of July we lost a child due to kwashiorkor, a disease caused by protein deficiency. Little Oskar had been stunted and wasted but did not exhibit the edema of face and extremities that was so evident in this child. Maria explained that, though the cause may be the same, the edema is one of the differences between Oskar's Marasmus and Kwashiorkor. Both diseases are the result of severe protein energy deficiency.

That child's was the first death that I had seen in mission and Maria immediately began dealing with the required items for the Afar custom of burial, which, in that climate, could not be postponed. She had previously laid in a bolt of undyed and unbleached fabric which would be used for a shroud. The Afar dig a hole about six feet deep. They are then obliged to tunnel in at a right angle at the bottom of the hole to form a cavity the right size for the body. The body is then slipped into this cavity and the hole filled. The use of the side tunnel prevents the hyenas and jackals from digging up the corpse. Women were not allowed at the funeral but I could see the mound of dirt covering the boy's grave from the lab.

Though the Afar in Gahla appeared to be in no immediate danger of famine, obviously that was not the case everywhere in the Afar region. The whole kebele (village) had walked all night to bring this child in, but it was too late. The little fellow was too far gone for any nutritional intervention to save him and we all felt the same frustration as we watched him sink into coma and death, his little body swollen and sad, and his grave was hard on the eyes.

I wondered where all that US aid was that we have read about being sent to Ethiopia. The truth is that much of it never makes it to the sick.

Only the Interest Payments Are Ongoing

Ethiopia is one of the largest recipients of foreign aid, $3 billion in 2008 alone, yet children still starve. Rona Peligal, on the website of Human Rights Watch, reports that "the Ethiopian government is routinely using access to aid as a weapon to control people and crush dissent. If you don't play the game, you get shut out. Yet foreign donors are rewarding this behavior with ever-larger sums of development aid." Farmers report being denied access to seed, micro-loans and fertilizer because they do not support the ruling party. Teachers in donor-supported schools report being threatened if they do not join the ruling party. Though donor officials told Human Rights Watch that they suspected donor programs were being used for political reasons, they had no way of knowing the extent of the abuse as monitoring is done jointly with Ethiopian government officials.

Nor is the abuse of aid funds in Ethiopia and other parts of Africa noticed only by Human Rights Watch. Steve Karlen wrote an article called "Africa Needs Democracy as Much as Debt Relief,"[3] in which he states that "The greatest source of Africa's problems exists in its political leadership, not lack of aid [per se] from the G8 nations." He shows how World Bank and International Monetary Fund loans to African governments far too often do not improve the lives of citizens but have added enormous debt to successive governments in the form of

3 In *The Capital Times* (Madison, Wisconsin), July 27, 2005, reprinted in *World Hunger*, op. cit.

compounding interest. Some developing country analysts say that the kinds of programs that the IMF imposes are unhelpful in themselves by undermining the local economy; and it is understood that often the loan mainly goes to pad politicians' pockets. Mr. Karlen goes on to say that the African Union itself, of which Ethiopia is a part, estimates that corruption costs the continent $148 billion each year, enough to wipe out the loan debt in just over two years. Though Ethiopia is technically a democracy, in 2005, after the election, there were mixed reviews on how fair that election was. Human Rights Watch reports that World Bank and other donors suspended direct budget support due to a crackdown by the government on demonstration's that left, "two hundred people dead and 30,000 detained." But the EU and the US Dept. of State deemed the election generally valid and aid soon recommenced, going this time to the nine district governments, where it would be even more diffused and harder to track. Much as we want to help, perhaps we should earmark some of the money to a supervision program. I would like to have tracked any aid meant for the Afar.

Laboratory Experiments in the Kitchen

Our cook had not yet returned from his self-scheduled R&R, and Maria and I were left to fend with dinner. Maria tried to fry rice but it scorched so she decided to make fried bread. She was beginning this task when I noticed that she was uncharacteristically quiet and asked her if she felt OK. She admitted that she was not feeling well. MSF had provided large containers with filters from which we were to procure all our drinking water. We were all diligent about filling our gourds from these containers. However, it was too little prophylaxis or too late. The kitchen girls washed dishes in two plastic tubs like children's wading pools. The water was too infrequently changed and, though we had soap and encouraged its use, there were no suds evident. Part of the problem was lack of language. We had two interpreters in camp that we relied upon to explain our wishes to the kitchen help as well as to everyone else, but the interpreters were needed in the clinic and hospital tents during the day, so we struggled to get points across with sign language and repetition when interpreters were absent. We have all heard the expression "lost in translation." Soap, fresh hot water and germ theory got lost somewhere. Organisms that the Afar were accustomed to and that probably did not make them sick were not so harmless to us. If hands were not washed when meals were prepared these organisms could be spread via the food or on dishes washed in contaminated water. I did a wet prep of Maria's stool and saw Giardia cysts in the microscope field. Giardia is a one-celled parasite found in the US, too, and, though it causes diarrhea, in a healthy person it is not life threatening. But, for Maria, coupled with the intense heat and what was probably recurring exposure, it was debilitating. We did have the medicine to treat the condition, but she had experienced a bad reaction to Metronidazole previously and did not want to take it. We insisted that she lie down and rehydrate.

I fried the dabo. It was edible, barely. The girls served the rice, regardless of scorch. It was a poor meal but at least it was different from the hideous macaroni that the cook had taken to preparing when we complained about non-stop spaghetti. The spaghetti was repetitive but well flavored. The macaroni was bland, of poor quality and extremely starchy. I couldn't get it down. It occurred to me that we might all have Giardia. That would account for the weight loss; but so could the macaroni. For whatever reason, I could feel my ribs for the first time in twenty years.

Jose and his crew were building permanent quarters for the staff at a greater distance from the hospital tents. The wooden buildings would be on stilts (less concern about snakes and spiders) and on a little rise to take advantage of any breeze. The pilings were in but, before he could continue on that task, we had the imperative job of getting Maria out of the patient kitchens. Her entreaties had been heard and MSF was to send a large quantity of supplies which we had to be able to store before we could start dispensing them to the patient families. We would still keep native staff to cook for the hospitalized patients in the event that there was no one else to cook for them, but once supplies were received; our staff would no longer cook for families or for patients who had family members to prepare their food. Jose put a rush on getting a storage shed completed. Poles arrived from Addis and corrugated metal sheets and another pole barn rose up from the desert to stand beside the patient cook shack and the thatched structure used to shelter the vehicles.

The day after the supplies arrived, medicine took a back seat to organizational work. There were burlap sacks of meal, cotton sacks of flour, bags of lentils, boxes of powdered milk and drums of oil. Every item was counted and stacked with others of its kind. We all got involved, expat staff, kitchen workers, patient families and even secondary treatment TB patients. Maria was in charge, counting every plastic plate and bowl and every metal cooking pot and tea kettle. There would be a dispensing of those items to each patient family and that family would then be responsible for preparing their own meals and those of their loved one in treatment.

Along with the supplies my long awaited barrel had arrived from Addis. I had given Fred the specifications for a WHO-approved waste burning barrel from the data I had in the lab and they brought it up the next day. We would no longer have to worry about goats or patients getting into the sputa.

One man named Urdu who had non-pulmonary tuberculosis was indefatigable, fetching and carrying with a will. Our drinking water came from our new well but it was stored in bladders as big as a king sized mattress. Urdu could be depended upon to fill the workers' gourds from the bladders, keeping them hydrated. He was a nice looking man but slight and very quiet. I often felt that he kept going out of sheer determination rather than physical strength. I brought Urdu to mind later on when some of the Afar grumbled about having to cook their own food, even though the ingredients had been handed to them. At the same time Vinod, our doctor, was out there rolling barrels of oil into place in order to feed them and Maria unpacked seemingly endless utensils with the sweat running down her young face and soaking her hair. The truth was that the Afar, like any other group of people, had their givers and their takers. I was grateful for the ones like Urdu who was smart enough to know that we were trying to help him and to show his appreciation in any way he could, most commonly by filling "gourds."

Jose had bought flower seeds during his break in Addis. I think he wanted to brighten our lives and he and Vinod decided to make flower beds in front of the lab. Unfortunately, Jose had bought varieties which would have grown beautifully in the comfortable climate of Addis. They had little chance in Gahla. At first, it seemed some stalwart seed must survive out of the fourteen packets of seeds they used in just two flower beds with dimensions of three by eight feet. All hope was dashed when our native gardener who was hired to work the vegetable garden decided that the beds needed more water. They were raised beds, surrounded by wooden rails, and he proceeded to hook up the hose to the pump on the well, and blasted seeds, soil and all hope of flowers out of those beds in just a few minutes time. It was another case of non-communication.

I had been in mission about six weeks when the water I drank began to come back up. I didn't understand it but I didn't feel any worse than usual, so I just plugged on as the rest of the team was doing. I had been taking pictures ever since the beginning of my journey. I had photographed the Afar, Fred in the office, Milton with the goat, Maria with Oskar, Jose wiring the laboratory, and after getting photos of Vinod and Jose planting the unfortunate flower beds, I realized that I didn't have any pictures of Vinod being a doctor. I told him that his parents did not send him to medical school to plant flower beds and I proceeded to follow him around, when I wasn't busy, taking pictures when appropriate. I never took pictures of the native people before asking their permission. The sign language for that was straight forward. I had snapped a few photos in the beginning that Vinod had taken to Addis for developing. After the local people saw their likenesses, I would just hold up the camera in a questioning gesture and they were almost all eager to have their picture taken.

One memorable picture I still have is of Medina, a stately looking lady who came to visit me at the lab. She was of middle age and was in mission accompanying her mother, a fact I got from sign language when she used a graphic whooshing motion from between her legs followed by a baby in arms sign, pointing to herself. She was very interested in my pictures of family that I had pinned up in the lab. Most of my family is blond and most of the pictures involved water, having been taken when we were snorkeling or poolside. I tried to explain the relationships, using the babe in arms motion for my grown children. I think she understood but her reaction was surprising. She smiled but seemed incurious as to the settings. She posed demurely when I took her picture and went her way, slim, graceful, self-composed.

The adult Afar never seemed to be curious about our way of life or envious of it. For centuries they had been convinced of their own strength, their superiority within their world. In one way it must have been a comfort to grow up believing you have it all. They are so far removed from civilization that they aren't exposed to temptation from TV ads and wealth displayed by others. In another way, this complacency serves to keep the unhealthy traditions alive, like that of encouraging marriage among first cousins. They resisted changes to their diets which would have been much to their advantage. The children loved fruit and took to it happily when Fred or one of the national staff brought oranges or mangos, but the adults never made the effort to travel to locations where it might be available even though, by working for MSF, many of them had cash to spend.

What the Afar women did have was an enviable sisterhood. I had read about their culture in advance so I was not surprised when I saw men holding hands. It was a simple gesture of affection. The women also held hands and kissed on the lips in greeting. They often smiled at each other, helped one another with tasks and took obvious delight in the company of other women. I suppose that being excluded from so many functions reserved only for men, it was natural to cling to their own gender. Maria found that she had to perform all internal exams on the women who were having difficult pregnancies. The male doctors were obliged to ask the male relative for permission to examine his wife or daughter. If the woman was near death, permission was sometimes given, but often it was not; so it became a three way consultation, with Maria doing the exam, telling the doctor what she found and the doctor giving her instructions. The women accepted all this and viewed life in general with great patience. I never saw the competition between women that raises its ugly head in the Western workplace. Since they appeared to be of little value in the general scheme of things, they took their value from each other.

In the lab, our microscopes were busier than ever. We still broke for several hours during the heat of the day but we were able to read longer in the morning, since we were no longer dependent on the sun, and there was one day we had six positives out of ten smears. We all said the same thing, "What are we going to do with them all?" Jose was very busy paying men and women to build deboiters as fast as possible since every TB patient had a retinue and they all had to be housed and fed. The staff compound, too, became more crowded. We had always had Kadir and Hassan, the native nurses, Ayub and Hiyu who wore many hats, the cook and four aides, including Adais and Hammadou as well as two others, but these were now augmented by men hired to supervise the work on the crew quarters. Afars like Mohammed headed building crews and we also had a Somali who did the same work. Camp became noisier, too, since the chewing of kaat was enjoyed by most if not all of these people. We began to see the downside of this habit. Hammadou liked to sit up late chewing and was often slow in the morning. There were men working for MSF as day laborers who lived in the surrounding deboiters and we saw evidence that some of these men beat their wives in their overexcitement, or perhaps there were arguments about where the money went. The drug, with its stimulant effects, suppressed appetite and kept the men even thinner than they would ordinarily have been. The old adage about "what goes up must come down" was at work and we saw the aftereffects of depression and fatigue. We all expressed concern that the money MSF was paying out to native employees was not making life better for the people in the settlement; but we had to have assistance. My tent had been propped up after the storm but the rain fly was hopeless. The permanent quarters were far from finished and Jose was obliged to throw up something in the meantime to shelter us from the coming rain.

In response to Jose's request for meat, Maria arranged with a restaurant in the nearest village of Mille to cook tibs for us. They were little ribs of salted goat meat, served with injera. The injera was very sour but the meat tasted good. I was sure it tasted even better to the young men of our group. Vinod was beginning to look like a sick Afar with his dark pinched face. I knew he had to feel the weight of being the only doctor in mission, but he worked tirelessly.

Quakers are nominally Christian but I wonder about those Christians who loudly extoll their superiority and attempt to force their narrow views on everyone else. I worked for two Hindu doctors in the US and found them to be the same kind of caring people as Vinod.

Alas for Ali

After we had the microscopes equipped with dependable light, I thoroughly checked the work of Ali, the tech who had been brought to us by our native nurse, Hassan. It was unavoidably apparent that he had a vision problem. I gave the same slides to both Ali and Hammadou after I had screened them myself. Hammadou did not miss one but Ali, despite taking a great deal of time to search, missed two out of five positives. I so dreaded having to tell the group that he would not work out; but I could not in all good conscience let him make the decisions for treatment when he was missing close to half of the positive slides. Neither would he be able to see the malaria parasite, which is even smaller. I told Vinod, who was very disappointed. He had hoped to have this professional tech to work while I was away on break. A meeting was called of the medical team and held in the dining area. Hassan and Ali were present and it was with a heavy heart that I explained the situation. Jose was kind enough to interpret so that we could keep the discussion among ourselves. Ali admitted that he had experienced some vision problems but he hadn't realized that it would affect his work. Everything was very civilized, but I was sorry when Ali said that he would return home. I knew that I had done the right thing for the patients, but I also knew that it was a disappointment for the Afar staff who wanted to have educated role models on site for the tribe.

Chapter 5. Birds and Beasts

Despite the dust storms, we had received very little total rain in Gahla. The native plants were used to making do with little, however, and the acacias were beginning to show green. More birds were showing up even in the barren area outside the lab. The sandgrouse were still plentiful, birds that I hadn't noticed at first because they were so well camouflaged by their gray and buff feathers. We had both Lichtenstein's and the Chestnut-bellied Sandgrouse. Even a birder had to think that they looked plump and meaty, especially a protein-deprived birder. In fact, one day, one of our trucks hit a sandgrouse and Fred, not wanting to waste any living thing, asked the cook to fix it for us. It was delicious but we didn't want to kill more of them. It wasn't the MSF way to eat the wildlife and it might have upset our hosts, who would never have thought of eating such a thing. For my part, I didn't want to scare the birds by plundering among them. As it was, the birds were not wary. It was easy to spot a Hueglin's Bustard, a bird nearly three feet tall which reminded me of our Sandhill Cranes, even to the face pattern. With more birds, there were bound to be more scavengers and one day an Egyptian Vulture lit not far from the lab, feeding on some animal that hadn't made it through the dry season. It was small compared to our Black or Turkey Vultures, as would be expected in an area where food might get scarce.

When at last I gathered my energy and went back to the river I could see that it was raining in the highlands because the river was rising. There were fewer sandbars and the plovers were moving to higher ground. I saw a Yellow-billed Stork, a smaller cousin of the Maribou. Yellow-billed Storks are considered a waterside species so I could see that I was in for more bird species as the season got wetter. On the same day, while I was sitting quietly, a low gurgling call captured my attention and I found a White-browed Coucal, a heavy skulking bird of the same family as the cuckoos. Another day when I was sitting on the sharp edge of the bank which had been carved by the swelling river, I glanced down between my feet to find a Hoopoe, close enough to touch though I didn't move a muscle. This bird, more than any other, symbolizes Africa to me. Though he was superficially like a very long-billed woodpecker and flew with the same undulating flight, that high Mohawk of feathers, his arrogant and deliberate march across the sand and the dizzying feather pattern of his wings puts the Hoopoe in a class by itself. Indeed it is the only member of its genus

I began to go to the river later in the evening. The hyenas never put in an appearance though I had heard them in the past. I also heard the jackals, a canine yip, unlike the hyenas. Hyenas are said to be more closely related to cats than to dogs. I might have mistaken their sounds for particularly loud birds had the Afar not known the sound well. They avoided the hyenas because they not only threatened livestock but had also been reported to attack people. In Harar, which was just south of us, the residents were so distraught by hyenas' attacks that they decided in the 1960s to pacify the hyenas by feeding them. First they made garbage available but since then, at least one man in the village has taken on the job of feeding hyenas scraps of meat. Originally the purpose was to keep them away from the livestock but it has since become a kind of tourist show. No one in Gahla was feeding hyenas voluntarily.

Milton had assured me that, despite the hyenas, the only danger was from the wild hogs. He had warned me not to go to the river at night but I thought I was OK in the evening as long as I left at dusk. The heat was less enervating later in the day and more birds came to drink. Insects were still active and the bee-eaters were after them. The Carmines were still around though they seemed to have finished nesting. There was also the White-throated Bee-eater, trailing an even longer split tail than the Carmine's. In July, the assumedly migratory Madagascar Bee-eater showed up, not a brilliant color like the Carmine, but a very pleasing mossy green with the black line through the eye that seems to be common to all the Bee-eaters. Another group of birds vying for insects were the Woodpeckers. The trees around the river were home to the Cardinal Woodpecker and to the Buff-spotted Woodpecker, both brown with red rather than black with red but otherwise similar to our Hairy and Downy Woodpeckers respectively. Not like any of our woodpeckers was the Red and Yellow Barbet, a different family but with zygodactyl toes like a woodpecker, an arrangement with one toe behind and the others foreword that allows the bird to cling to a tree trunk rather than perching on a limb. The Barbet gets your attention with a bright yellow body, red face with white ear, body spots and nose hairs.

There were peculiar insects in mission also. I had seen tumble bugs on the farm in Indiana, small dung beetles about half an inch long that roll cow dung into marble sized balls and then use the balls as a nest for their young. In the Danakil we had dung beetles two inches long with large thick bodies, that rolled up goat and cow dung into tennis size balls. These dung beetles were the scarabs of ancient Egypt. The Egyptians believed that a huge dung beetle rolled the sun across the sky as these insects rolled their dung. When Kadir first told me that the custom of female circumcision came from the pharaohs, it seemed to me that Egypt was too far away to have influenced the Ethiopian way of life; but here were beetles known in Egypt. In fact only the Sudan lies between Ethiopia and Egypt and the Afar have roamed North Africa for centuries.

Another member of the scarab family was the Rhinoceros Beetle, a big black insect with a hard curving horn arising from the top of his head. The beetles can lift each other and the males compete by doing just that. The beetle that is tossed is the loser.

One evening after the rains started, as we were sitting on the mats after dinner, a number of the native staff jumped up and began running around swatting the ground viciously, shouting to each other in their language. Our expat team could only look on in wonder and shrug at each other ignorantly until the men could take time to show us the intruder. Kadir held up the carcass of an insect three inches long which they called a camel spider—but which looked like a scorpion to me. I later found that they are Arachnids but are also called Wind Scorpions because their legs are clustered at either end of elongated bodies, making them look more like scorpions. We were warned that they could get as big as six inches and could inflict a painful bite. They were incredibly fast and dun colored. The spiders liked drier areas and must have been fleeing from the river area which was getting wetter. We were told that they would not purposely seek us out but would defend themselves if cornered and any bite was likely to become infected.

More birds were showing up outside the lab. I had previously identified the Golden Pipit which I thought of as a brighter Dickcissel, roughly the same size and with a black napkin. After the season began to change, a bird appeared that turned out to be the Abyssinian Longclaw. This bird was remarkably like our Meadowlarks though it is not even in the same family. There were two birds occupying the same niche and with the same markings but half a world apart; an example, I believe, of convergent evolution, whereby organisms develop similar appearances in order to take advantage of similar environments, though they may not be related to each other. It was a pleasure to see the bird's brilliant yellow breast beautifying our barren space.

After the planting of the flower beds, Jose had asked staff to build a fence around the lab so as to keep the goats out of the flowers. The fence, a somewhat flimsy structure made out of fallen Acacia branches, would probably not have deterred the goats if the flowers had indeed come up. At least the moist ground drew insects, and that increased our bird species. I had looked forward to the African Starlings which are well known for their beauty. We had the Purple Starling, which cannot be properly described with one color. The feathers are iridescent and, though the breast is purple, the back is an equally scintillating green and the eye is bright yellow. Another of the Glossy Starling family was the Lesser Blue-eared Starling, with a blue belly and a stripe through the yellow eye. These knock-out birds kept company with the Common Bulbuls, brownish birds whose only color was the yellow on the undertail. They made up for their lack of flashy hues with so many noise variations that the description of their call took up five lines in the bird book. As the flying insects increased I began to see swallows, the Ethiopian Swallow, very like our Tree swallow and the African Sand Martin, a plain little bird with a tiny bill.

The Abyssinian Roller is a stocky bird of an overall swimming pool blue when perched but flaunting a brown back when in flight along with royal blue epaulets. The rollers are named for their agile flight displays. They eat insects or vertebrates and perch in plain sight, like the one that I saw as I approached the river at twilight. I was prepared to sit awhile as I was hoping to see night birds. Though I had dimly seen nighthawks flitting overhead while searching the skies in the evening, I could not identify the species and the nightjars remained one family of birds that I had not been able to list. I did not want to miss anything so I stayed at the river one evening later than before. I used my flashlight to search the trees, hoping to catch the reflective eyes of the Ethiopian birds as we do the Paraques in the American Southwest. It was chance, however, and not the flashlight that got me a Slender-tailed Nightjar as he rested on a low branch before venturing out to catch insects on the wing.

On the way back to camp, I knew that I had done exactly what Milton had warned me not to do. I had stayed out long enough to see the hogs. Warthogs are not the cute and clumsy beasts of Lion King. I paused as I saw in my peripheral vision a large hog who was watching me closely, like a sentry. In the failing light, I glimpsed other hogs moving behind it. My reference insisted that Warthogs are active in the daytime but these animals, probably due to the excessive heat of the day, came out in the evening. He or she was perhaps fifty yards away, a dark squatty body with the curving tusks clearly visible. I was just brave enough to click one picture before easing on my way.

One day I was followed when I went to the river. A little boy of ten years or so joined me as though he had been watching for me to pass. The kids were beginning to pick up rudimentary English and I was able to ascertain that his name was Ali. Ali reached for my gourd, tugging on it to show me that he wanted me to take it off my shoulder. My first thought was that he was thirsty, though I had just seen him come from the village area where water was available. I was asking myself whether I should let him drink from my gourd, ignoring health concerns in this land of endemic TB, or risk hurting his feelings by refusing. I decided I'd rather risk infection than leave a child thirsty. But Ali didn't want to drink. He just wanted to carry my gourd. I then wondered whether he expected to be paid, cynical as we Westerners tend to be. Ali didn't expect to be paid either. He just wanted to do something nice for the foreign woman who liked the birds. I shared my binoculars with him and he was excited to see the Sunbirds close up, four varieties present at that time.

The Sunbirds in Africa fill the niche of our Hummingbirds. They hang from blossoms and feed on nectar. The acacias were finally flowering and the first species we saw was the Beautiful Sunbird which looked black until the light from the sun could be diffracted by his feathers. Then he twisted about the blossom in all his glory, glistening green head and back, butter yellow sides, and when he worked his way to the back side of the bush, photons exposed his bright red belly. The Black-bellied Sunbird joined him, with similar red and green but instead of yellow sides, he was accessorized with blue. Most of the Sunbirds that I saw in mission measured about five inches from tip of bill to tip of tail and had long curving bills with which to gather nectar. The Pygmy Sunbird is smaller, though the male develops an extended tail in breeding season. It was interesting that the female Sunbirds, like our female Hummers, were plain brown with perhaps a little yellow and were hard to tell apart. Again nature has made sure that the mother bird is not conspicuous on her nest. She may have been less beautiful to our eyes but all the preening and posturing of the male was done in her honor.

Looking out the window of the lab during this season, my eyes beheld an Afar herdsman leading all the camels to a greener section by the river. It looked like something from Lawrence of Arabia, this long train of camels; big males, smaller females and the youngsters, clomping along in single file followed by a native man in his kurta, driving them on; an "I really am in Africa" moment.

Though camels and goats provided most of the meat and milk used by the Afar, there were some cattle. They were pitiful beasts, bony and slow, suffering in the climate and close to starvation but there are individualists among the Afar as there are among any group and a few of the men chose to keep cattle. National Geographic offers computer wallpaper depicting Zebu cattle of the Afar region being herded through a dusty cracked landscape even more barren than Gahla. The Brahmin cattle we have in Florida are a type of Zebu, the different breeds of which have humps and dewlaps. The cattle in Gahla did not have prominent humps. They may have been mixed but I believe that the cattle in mission were at least partly descended from a long horned humpless breed that was established in Egypt more than 2000 years ago and which migrated south over time. The Red-billed Oxpecker rode around on the backs of the cattle and camels gleaning ticks. He was a fairly large bird of about eight inches, closely matching the color of his brownish hosts except for the red bill and the large yellow ring around his red eye.

Chapter 6. Addis; Getting the Big Picture

The Afar people, despite the heat and primitive lifestyle, did not smell. They washed in the river often, though the women never undressed but instead walked into the water with clothes on and washed modestly beneath their skirts. As the river rose, our medical team began to worry about Schistosomiasis or, as the native staff called it, Bilharziosis, the parasitic disease previously mentioned, that could come from bathing in water which contained the host snails. Vinod wanted to be sure that we would be able to inspect the urine of patients suspected of having the disease since the parasite comes in through the urethra and eventually lodges in the bladder.

I was ill prepared for performing that test as I had only seen pictures of the organism but decided that, like any solid in urine, the organisms should be visible if spun down by gravity in a centrifuge and the sediment viewed under a microscope. The MSF lab kit had contained a hand cranked centrifuge and I caught some urine and set Hammadou and Adais to cranking. Though they took turns cranking madly, laughing as young men do when competing against each other, the gears slipped and we could not get a proper sedimentation. No patient had come forth with the symptoms at that time so I didn't have to worry yet about being able to find the one celled culprit. I set that problem on the shelf for the time being and concentrated on making sure that my two helpers could handle the TB slides while I was in Addis. We were seeing a 26% positive rate for our smears, an extremely high rate, so it wasn't difficult to find smears to use for teaching. I already knew that Hammadou was proficient at finding the bacteria and I was glad to see that Adais also checked out well when tested. Now there were two boys, without any written material, who had learned to stain, to measure, to use a microscope, an item they probably had never seen, and most surprising to me, to take their work seriously. They had to be commended for having the persistence to search each slide diligently and for never missing a scheduled day of work. I finally felt OK about leaving them in charge of patient smears and left for Addis on July 9.

The beginning part of our journey, overland, was by necessity slow and I got a chance to see birds, including a larger flock of Ostrich than we had seen before. An Abyssinian Scimitarbill was perched on a low branch and I spotted a Grey-backed Fiscal, a shrike very like our Loggerhead. Our highway route passed through Awash National Park. Though we did not have time to tour the park my driver did stop to allow me to photograph a group of Gelada baboons. They came out into the road and I could plainly see the "bleeding heart" red patch on the chest of the ranking male. Gelada baboons are unique to the Ethiopian highlands and are the last one left of the genus Theropithecus, the others having gone extinct. The other baboons emitted a sharp bark and hightailed it off the road when we stopped. The male stayed and his demeanor was menacing, teeth bared and long back fur puffed.

Where the river was near, a White-faced Whistling Duck flew over, trailing his long legs, an adaptation for roosting in trees. While many of the bird families I saw in Africa have members in North America, we in the US have only one species of the stork family, Ciconidiae. The Rift Valley had eight and picking his way amongst the brush was an Abdim's Stork. There was also a Grey Heron, a species so similar to our Great Blue Heron that I thought it was the same until I checked the reference.

Probably the most impressive mammal I was to see in Ethiopia was cresting the top of a hill as we were leaving the area of the park. I looked out to see a Beisa Oryx, a large antelope with very tall backward curving horns outlined against the sky. Overhead there was a huge Lappet-faced vulture, nearly twice the size of our Black Vultures but like our birds, a master at soaring.

As our elevation increased so did the grassland birds. Another small Francolin, Coqui's this time, darted among the brush. The Denham's Bustard then rewarded my persistence. The Denham's breeding male can't be missed with his large size, striped wings and an enormous white fluff of feathers covering his throat and breast.

I thought that I had come across a familiar bird, the Anhinga anhinga so common in our Florida ponds, but it was an African darter, Anhinga rufa, named for the reddish cast of its neck feathers. The behavior was similar, as I saw it perched with wings outspread over a small wetland. The lack of oil in the feathers makes it possible for anhingas to swim with only their heads above water, so it is easier for them to dive and spear their fish but also necessitates long periods of drying in the sun.

Ali, the tech with the vision problem accompanied us back to Addis. I hoped that he did not bear any resentment for being denied a job and indeed, he did not. He graciously invited me to dine with him in a Muslim restaurant in Nazret where we stopped for lunch. We did not share enough common language to actually converse but I did recognize a mural that appeared to be Mecca on the wall of the restaurant and he confirmed that it was indeed Mecca. The food was good, tibbs with rice, well spiced, but I was able to eat only a small amount. I couldn't understand what had happened to my appetite. After the half way switch Ali sat up front with the driver, an Orthodox Amhar from Addis, of approximately his age, and they seemed to have a good conversation. I couldn't understand the language, but I knew the words Christian and Muslim and could recognize the back-and-forth form of explanations—with no argument.

Cash Only and the Price is Always Questioned

Fred went with me to Addis and we stopped to buy what he called Pomcannelle, a warty fruit like a small pineapple with large seeds inside. The pulp around the seeds tasted like watermelon. The highlands were green and beautiful and the weather perfect. There were puddles but our driver told us that it only rained at night. I was eager to get my film developed so I hired a taxi to take me around. The taxi for the day cost me one hundred birr (a little over $12.00). This was not much had I had access to my funds, but Moussa had insisted that all expats leave both credit cards and passports in the safe at the Addis compound. He said it was for our safety and credit cards would not have been accepted at the vast majority of shops anyway. It did mean, however, that I had to be frugal with my cash. Joel, the doctor with whom I had shared the coffee ceremony, had asked me to exchange his birr for American bills when he was leaving and I had been glad to do so. That money was all I had, as our per diem had only been enough to pay for our food thus far.

While I was waiting for my film to be developed I realized that I was somewhat hungry. I went into a restaurant and ordered a hamburger, which was extremely well done and should not have made me ill. Nevertheless, while I was in the Fanco Market which served the needs of expats, I began to feel weak and dizzy. I was forced to limit the buying of food for myself and for my team and to go instead to the house and lie down. Terafou was away, visiting her relative, but I boiled my purchased chicken with carrots and potatoes and ate sparingly, hoping the good broth would be a tonic to my system. Little of it was retained, however. It was frustrating to me to be sick as I had always had a cast iron stomach.

The next day, despite aching joints and headache, I went to the Mercato, a large market area where I bought souvenirs for the smaller kids at home. In the afternoon Moussa had Solomon take me to buy fabric and curtain rods for the lab so we could shade the windows during the hottest part of the day. It was reassuring to have this competent man at my elbow. He did all the haggling and decided at the hardware shop how many rings we needed to hang the curtains. We had to go to a third shop to get the thread. The bazaar was a rabbit warren of shops. I would never have been able to find the right items without help. We then went to a furniture store and looked at stools to replace the homemade ones we were using in the lab. The stools were very plush and Solomon encouraged me to buy them for my comfort but they cost 1300 birr each, about $160.00. I could not justify that kind of expense; we went to a medical supply and bought stools without backs but still adjustable in height for 300 birr each. I knew the new stools would still be of great benefit to us, as my trainees and I had been obliged to use combinations of cushions to accommodate our different heights when using the microscopes.

Back at the house, I knew that I had overdone it. I was extremely tired and not able to eat at all. The next day I was forced to spend in bed. Terafou had returned and was worried enough about me to call the office. Dominique arrived to examine me, much to my embarrassment. I did not want to be a liability. He could see immediately that I was dehydrated but he felt that it was due to salt depletion rather than to lack of water since I was drinking regularly. He left some medication and advised me to drink the rehydration salts that we used for patients when I returned to mission.

That evening Chafika visited me, a young woman who had impressed me with her modernity during my first visit to Addis, but I opened the door that evening to a black-robed shape with only the eyes showing. She had adopted a black Muslim head covering and was even holding an edge of the filmy fabric across her lower face. I tried to hide my surprise but she broached the subject immediately. She said, "People assume that my parents forced me to take the veil but they left it entirely up to me." I did not get into the reasons for her choice that evening.

Chafika explained one of the Muslim beliefs to me. When I was showing her the pictures which I had taken when I first arrived in Ethiopia, one picture showed a dog who lived at the guest house. Chafika told me that Muslims consider dogs to be unclean. If a Muslim touches a dog he must wash his hands. They do not allow dogs to live in their houses and try to avoid them if possible. I was to remember this lesson later when the awful pictures came out portraying the abuse of Muslim soldiers in Guantanamo. Techniques used to break down resistance of prisoners and to obtain information included the exploitation of what the military called "phobias, such as fear of dogs" and the forcing of prisoners "to bark and perform dog tricks." At no time did I read or hear on the news that dogs were used because they were anathema to Muslims, taking advantage of Muslim prohibition. Those prisoners were not cringing because they were afraid of the dog. They were appalled at the offense to God.

Due to illness, I had missed my ride back to camp so had another day in Addis. The meds had helped and I walked to the office the next morning to read my e-mail. The gardens were striking after the bleakness of the desert and I spotted a Tacaze Sunbird searching the blooms of the bougainvillea and the pink trumpet vine. This Sunbird was nine inches long, much larger than the other members of the species that I had seen at mission. The larger size is due to the increased availability of food and is also associated with cooler climates. There was a Grey Woodpecker, very like our Red-bellied, on a eucalyptus tree, not a native tree to Addis but rather one of the progeny of trees brought from Australia. At my feet, rustling the few dried leaves not yet raked up by the industrious gardener was an Olive Thrush, a duller version of the American Robin.

I was anxious to see Lucy, the skeleton of one of humanity's ancient humanoid ancestors. Lucy is estimated to be three to four million years old and was found in the Awash valley of our very own Afar depression. Indeed, her proper name is Australopithecus afarensis. So, on my last day in Addis, I took a taxi to the National Museum of Ethiopia to visit Lucy, so called because the Beatles's song, *Lucy in the Sky with Diamonds* is said to have been playing on the boombox of the expedition at the time of discovery. The skeleton on view is a plaster replica and less than four feet long but it was interesting to know that the original walked the area close to mission on two feet and saw green forests around her and plenty of game. It seemed that I was the only visitor to the museum at that time.

I did not wish to return to mission without buying peanut butter, yogurt for Maria and the other niceties that other members of the team had brought from their trips to Addis. I took a taxi to the market and spent an hour there, but again began to feel weak. I hadn't eaten so I found a shop and ordered an omelet with bread and coffee. I could only eat part of it and put the bread in my purse. It was time to get another taxi to a book shop and it was a struggle on my own. They knew enough English to give me a price but if they told me 25 birr, they changed it to 35 when we had traveled only a very short distance. It was never the agreed upon sum. I would not have begrudged them the money but I did not have much cash by this time. I had asked Momin to buy four more *jiles* as gifts for relatives and friends back home. He was stunned, and when I handed him the cash, less than a hundred dollars worth, he looked as though he had never seen so much at one time. In retrospect, I think my action could be seen as the kind of crass money flashing that Americans have done around the world, especially since I knew that most Afar save for a long time to buy one jile. Though I meant no harm, it was the kind of move that draws uncomfortable attention to visitors to the developing world. If I walked down the street in Addis, there were people, especially children, importuning me for handouts. I grew weary of the shouted "feranji" (foreigner). The constant harassment was tiring.

The taxi driver I eventually procured stopped for gas, and while he was pumping it a little boy came up to my window. He rubbed his stomach and held out his hand. I had followed Veronique's advice up to this point and handed out my change to beggars since it was of small value to me and I didn't understand the denominations of the coins anyway. But, with no way of knowing when I would get more money, I couldn't give him what I had, so I just gave him the bread from my purse. The child consumed the bread like he had not eaten in days. He probably hadn't.

Aid for Whom?

The US is the world's largest international aid donor. The Congressional Budget gives the figure of $427,472,000 in aid to Ethiopia in 2009. Yet, MSF's latest campaign, Starved for Attention, concerns the lack of nutritional assistance to the developing world. MSF contends that "the world's top donors, including the United States, Canada, Japan, and the European Union, continue to supply and finance nutritionally substandard foods to developing countries, despite conclusive scientific evidence of their ineffectiveness in reducing childhood malnutrition." MSF International President, Dr. Unni Karunakara, says that," the vast majority of international food assistance programs rely on fortified blended flours such as corn-soya blend (CSB) cereals. CSB cereals do not meet international standards for the nutritional needs of children less than two years of age." Dr. Karunakara feels that we are using a double standard by sending foods that we do not feed to our own children for the use of children overseas. The campaign alludes to countries that have successfully reduced early childhood malnutrition such as Mexico, Thailand, the US and many European countries and how they focus on access to quality foods such as milk and eggs by poor families to maintain nutritional health. The US has sent milk as part of aid packages only to a few select countries in recent years, none of them Ethiopia. So, why not?

The answer begins with US agriculture. The food aid program came out of the Agricultural Act of 1949 when it was decided that surplus commodities produced in the US could be sent outside the US when the need arose as aid. It sounded like a good idea but forces have come to bear that make aid attractive to business. Today, there are no stocked surpluses. Instead, farm subsidies in the form of payments to more than 250,000 farmers cost the American taxpayers $5 billion a year in direct payments alone without counting the cost of price supports. The top 1% of recipients, large agricultural conglomerates, receive 17% of the payments which are given without consideration of need. Then, after the farmer has been encouraged to grow more than the US population can consume, the US buys back the subsidized grain in order to send it overseas as aid. Frederick Mousseau and Anuradha Mittal wrote in *The Humanist*, March/April 2006,[4] that a single US company, Horizon Milling, a joint venture of Cargill Inc., has sold to the US government $1.09 billion worth of grain for food aid operations, grain that was already subsidized. Cargill sales were in the range of $50 billion in 2004 and Cargill operates in over 160 countries — big business indeed.

The American system for delivering food aid is also unique. Other nations buy food locally wherever possible so as to avoid both shipping costs and the impact on the local economy. But the US buys the grain from US famers and then pays US shipping companies, and only US shipping companies, to carry it all over the world. Carolyn Gluck of Oxfam, says, "For roughly $1 spent on aid, the US taxpayer is paying $2 to get it there." These figures are supported by a report in the New York Times stating that the actual food delivered by the USA, via the

4 Reprinted in *World Hunger, op. cit.*

NGO's and the World Food Program that it uses for dispersal, was in value only 40% of the food aid budget. The rest went to costs involved with getting it to recipients. And not only is this system of shipping cost prohibitive, it is also slow. Chris Barnett, a development economics professor at Cornell told ABC news that "the median time to deliver aid from the US is just under five months.'

There is another side effect connected to our treatment of aid. When large amounts of food show up in an area for free, why would anyone buy the crops produced by local farmers? There are reports of Ethiopian grain rotting in warehouses while the local people are being fed, well or otherwise, on imported US grain. The beleaguered US taxpayer could have saved a bundle buying the Ethiopian grain and benefitted the Ethiopian farmer at the same time. This is not a new idea. Under increasing pressure to transform an inefficient system, George W Bush tried to get Congress to pass legislation allowing for one quarter of American emergency assistance to be delivered in cash instead of processed crop purchases. But Samuel Loewenberg, as published in *The Lancet* (May 6, 2006),[5] says the proposal "went nowhere. It was killed by agro-business, the shipping industry and the farm-state congressmen that control food aid." Finally, in 2008, Congress did allow for $60 million over the next four years to be spent on local and regional food purchases. Now the Obama administration has requested $300 million in International Disaster Assistance for an "emergency food security fund." This fund would enable aid officials to procure some food locally or regionally or to provide vouchers for local food when food is available but hungry people cannot afford to buy it.

That's good news but will it reach the people who are not close to markets? "Three fourths of the world's hungry are politically marginalized people who live in rural areas." says, Susan Sechler in *The American Prospect* (Winter 2002)[6]. Obviously, it takes a lot more effort to get relief supplies to a place such as Gahla, ten hours out of Addis, than to feed people within easy distance of the warehouse.

That brings up another issue involving the US practice of insisting on using US grain delivered by NGOs. According to Sophia Murphy

5 Reprinted in *World Hunger, op. cit.*
6 Reprinted in *World Hunger, op. cit.*

and Kathy McAfee in "U.S. Food Aid: Time to Get It Right," a paper published July, 2005, the US is by far the largest donor to the World Food Program but nearly all of that donation is in the form of food from the US. Also, three charities; CARE, World Vision, Catholic Relief Services and to a lesser extent, five others, received about 30% of the 1.5 billion of their total income in donated food in 2001. All of these organizations need cash in order to disperse the food and for other development projects. So they sell some of the food given as aid in cash markets. They would prefer not to do it this way. Other countries give them cash so they don't have to sell aid food, interfering with local economies and adding marketing costs but, with our insistence on sending grain from the US, they have little choice. This means that people who can afford to buy food get it right away in a local market while other hungrier people wait for the organization to procure the funds it needs to get the food aid to them. That explains why I saw bags stamped with "US Wheat" being sold as empty sacks in Addis while here was a child in the same capital city of Ethiopia who was obviously not getting food, let alone the right food.

MSF followed three mothers enrolled in the WIC program in the US. The WIC (Women, Infants and Children) program makes sure that juice, milk, cheese, eggs, legumes, fruits and vegetables as well as bread are supplied at no cost to any mother and child not able to afford them in the US. It is a necessary program that pays for itself. Vitamin deficiencies that were seen during the Depression are generally a thing of the past in America and mental retardation due to lack of protein is very rare.

In the developing world it is a different matter. Though protein-energy malnutrition ranks eighth on the leading causes of death in the African Region, reference the "WHO Media Center Fact Sheet" for 2002, it *contributes* to all of the first seven. When I look at the printout of the Special Nutritional Products used by the UN World Food Program, it would appear that 100 grams of "Corn-Soya Blend," provided by the US as aid, should provide about 18 grams of protein, enough to satisfy the minimum daily requirement for a small child. So why does MSF feel that the food is inadequate? The primary reason is because a two-year-old can't eat it. For one thing, 100 grams is one-fourth of a whole box of shredded wheat. CSB is usually made into a thin gruel, giving it even more bulk. When a child is very malnourished, he can eat only a very small amount at a time. That small amount must be of the highest nutritive value. CSB, according to Sophie Delaunay, Executive Director of MSF/USA, is "high in anti-nutrients, inhibiting proper digestibility and absorption. It contains no dairy products, important for growth." Conversely, Ready-To-Use Foods (RUTFs), such as Plumpy Nut bars, recommended for malnourished toddlers, contain peanuts, sugar, milk powder, vegetable oil, vitamins and minerals and are easy to eat.

If we are spending billions in food aid and the UN says that 11,000 children die from malnutrition every day, something is awry. Maybe we should end subsidies, let the market decide how much grain US farmers should grow and try buying dried milk and eggs as well as fortified cereals closer to the target location of hungry kids. Likely, some food will always need to be imported. US companies could still participate in food aid programs but in a way that supplies the most nutrition by weight. Recently, a California dairy company began making bars similar to Plumpy Nut (but without peanut butter) that have been approved by UNICEF.

It is also time to stop outdated aid to select US shippers. In 2002, Barrett and Maxwell, a large public accounting firm, found that only thirteen US shippers were approved to ship US food for aid. That number is down from eighteen shippers the year before. Lack of competition has increased cost. Few US shippers are benefitting from our policy of restricting shipment of aid to US firms but the inefficiency of getting food to the hungry is greatly increased by the same requirement. This kid in Addis wasn't a toddler. He was probably nine or ten years old and could probably have eaten a quarter box of cereal had it been available. Maybe it was still on the ship coming from America.

After the incident with the boy, I decided to give up on the reading material and my demanding taxi driver, and to ride the bus home. I transferred myself to the curb at the bus terminal and waited a long time but the correct bus did not appear. Out of the crowd came three well, though conservatively, dressed women with no head coverings, Orthodox. I think some of my companions on the curb had fetched them. They informed me that I had been waiting on the wrong side.

They then insisted on putting me on the correct mini taxi where I hit another snag when the fare was 90 cents and I had only 80 cents and a 100 birr note which the driver couldn't change. Again I was saved by a fellow passenger who said she was a student in California but home on holiday. She kindly kicked in the 10 cents difference and helped me to find my stop.

Dominique came again to see me that evening along with a new arrival, Anne Marie, of France. She was a midwife eager to go on to the hospital at Dubti. By that time, I had rested and told Dominique that I would return to mission the next day. Dominique mentioned that a mission further west in Ethiopia had doubts about their technician and hoped that I would consent to visiting them before I left for home to check his work. I told him that I would be glad to do so if I could be replaced at Gahla. Dominique "sweetened the pot" by promising that, if I went, he would make sure that a stop was made on the way. I would get to see the famed churches of Lalibela, hewn from solid rock and either standing below ground level or chiseled into the mountain side. Of course, I wanted to see Lalibela but I was also thinking of the wetter, upland location of that mission and all those new species of birds.

Chapter 7. The Lab Burgeons

I had not expected to find the return to mission taxing. Essentially nothing had changed. However, I felt weak to the point of passing out in the heat of the afternoon. We were to move into our new shelters and my team had waited for me to move my things. I did so at once so that my pitiful sagging tent could be put to rest. Our shelters consisted of a framework with a thatched roof over blue plastic, walled and divided into two parts with mats. Jose had found some dark gravel for the floors. Maria and I would sleep in one side and Vinod, Jose and Fred in the other. The native medical staff also had a shelter. My mattress had gotten wet and I now had a new one with a plastic cover.

Vinod confirmed that Hammadou and Adais had performed their duties well in my absence. Adais was not his perky self, however. He came to me just before dinner to tell me that he didn't feel well. That proved to be an understatement as his skin was burning when I touched his forehead. We went immediately to the lab where I pricked his finger and stained the smear which teemed with the distinctive rings of malaria parasites, often two in one red cell. These rings exhibited double red dots. The whole picture was diagnostic for P. falciparum. When I was a student and learning the types of malaria over thirty years ago, my mnemonic for the variety of malaria from which Adais was suffering, was "falciparum is fatal." It was always fatal at that time and is still responsible for the vast majority of malarial deaths. Fortunately, we now had the drugs to counteract it if it had not gone too far. Adais had told Vinod that he was sick the previous week but described it as a gastrointestinal upset and did not tell him that it was a recurring fever. Perhaps he had become accustomed to the idea of using the lab to diagnose but malaria has been treated for years just on the basis of symptoms. The maturation of the parasites in the patient's red blood cells occurs at predictable intervals, precipitating shivers and chills when the red cells rupture and release their toxic contents. In general, P. falciparum causes an attack of shivering about every two days while P. vivax matures every three days. Vinod started him on Fansidar, which was the most reliably effective drug in our area of Africa, and we all hoped disaster was averted.

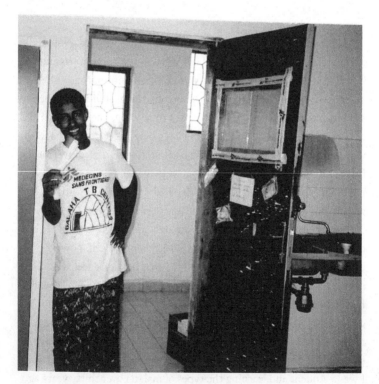

The malaria parasite, Plasmodium falciparum for one, is carried by the female Anopheles mosquito. In mission, as the season became wetter, the mosquitoes increased and the malaria followed. The cycle, abbreviated, is this: when the mosquito bites, it transfers the parasite to the human host where the organism sets up housekeeping in the human liver. It waits there to infect red blood cells as they pass through that organ. The organism matures within the RBCs until it is ready to multiply, at which time the red cells break open spilling infective merozoites into the blood. Since many red cells are infected at the same time, many of them lyse (break) at the same time and the body reacts to this intrusion, resulting in the terrible chills with fever that rack the infected patient, these rigors sometimes lasting for hours. Since we did not want to miss any cases, I had worked to perfect my thick smears using larger drops of blood and the Wright stain without the fixative so as to lyse the red cells on the slide rather than preserving them for study as we do in ordinary blood smears. Increasing the number of red cells would increase the likelihood of finding the malaria organisms which remain on the slide undamaged after the red blood cell is destroyed by the lysing agent. However, I soon found that the parasites were usually so prevalent that I could see them in a thin smear, easily visible inside the intact red cells. The book said that P. vivax was found in our area as well as P. falciparum but what I found was falciparum. Seeing the affected patients gripped in the paroxysms of fever made us all aware of our vulnerability. I was disappointed to read that the Larium I was taking would not keep me from getting malaria. It would only keep it from developing into complications. We all began to use the insect repellant that had been supplied, but it wasn't our familiar Off. It was a Vaseline-based goo that melted in the heat and closed the pores of the skin so that we felt hotter than ever.

The curtain rods were installed in the lab and Maria had arranged for a local tailor to hem the tops. I chose to wash the fabric before the bottom was hemmed to allow for shrinkage and to do the final hemming myself. While in the lab, stitching, I had to rescue a gecko and put him outside and chase down a camel spider. I assumed the gecko was a harbinger of wetter weather, which would be welcome to the Afar, but I did not appreciate another invader in the laboratory.

Our patient load was booming and the number of deboiters had tripled since I had first come to mission. A third hospital tent was being erected at a distance from the others to be used strictly for TB patients. It was on a slight rise so it got better ventilation. Close by were the new teams' living quarters, sturdy structures already standing on their pilings. We all went down one evening to examine the new complex and complimented Jose on the progress he and his workers had made, though we knew that the shelters would not be done before we all left mission. Priority had to be given to tents, supply sheds and deboiters. More patients meant more smears and Vinod informed me that one of the interpreters, Ayub, wanted to train in the lab. He didn't really have a medical background but I knew he was bright, and Hammadou was on break so I did need the help. A new trainee, Aden, was to begin training as well. He was an aide in the hospital tents as Hammadou and Adais had been, and he was married, with a child, and seemed very motivated. Since Ayub spoke excellent English, it would be easy to explain the techniques.

However, it took only two days to get an impression of Ayub. He was sloppy and threw matches on the floor. His habit of chewing kaat until late at night made him something of a "space cadet." He would zone out over a smear and take forever to finish it. It was not a problem for him to find the organisms when he was paying attention, but I never knew whether he had thoroughly searched the slide in the grid pattern necessary so as not to miss low level incidence. Aden, on the other hand, did very well and I trusted his work. I had been planning to show my trainees some basic lab tests beyond staining such as a White Blood Cell Count and stool analysis, so I decided that rather than reject Ayub entirely I would keep him on and use him to interpret when Hammadou came back from break.

Friends, With and Without Feathers

More fruit was available now from outside settlements and one day after lunch I mixed some of the oranges and mangoes that had been brought as supplies with the coconut that I had bought in Addis. It wasn't a good grade of coconut and we were missing the other ingredients of Ambrosia but the entire staff, Afar as well as expat, trooped in to have a little bowl of my concoction and enjoyed it very much. I was glad to return a little of the hospitality that had been shown to me.

We were now in our shelters, which were cooler than the tents, though the mosquito net that I was now obliged to use acted to shut off much of the air that might have found its way in. It was a circular contraption with a ring at the top and wooden spokes to make it fan out all around my mattress. The net could then be tucked in underneath. I knew it was necessary but, between the net at night and the greasy repellent during the day, I had developed a heat rash. My skin had always been sensitive and it had finally rebelled. I did enjoy having Maria for my roommate, though. We lay at night in the darkness and shared our doubts and hopes. Maria seemed to make decisions easily and to stick by them but in the privacy of our shelter, she admitted to wondering about this or that policy and I tried to give her my take on the situation. There were issues with the Afar men and their macho attitude, team relations, the supply problems. She also worried about me and told me that even the cook knew that I didn't like the food. I found this embarrassing as I have never been a picky eater. I tried to explain that it wasn't that I didn't like the food. I simply had no appetite. I certainly did not want to be another problem. She had more than enough. Maria, young as she was, had the responsibility of close to eighty working people who were not only practicing medicine but also building deboiters and crew quarters, growing gardens, doling out foodstuffs and getting supplies. Had I been in her shoes, heavy would have been the crown.

At the river, the rise in the water level was stunning. The sandbars were gone and the current was swift. The Black-headed heron, another bird similar to our Great Blue, made his appearance as well as the Striated Heron, very like our Black-crowned Night Heron. Many birds were completely new. There was a Black-crowned Tchagra, a member of the family of Bush-Shrikes, a family we don't have in North America. And a Pygmy Batis, a tiny bird that gleaned insects from foliage as well as darting out for flying insects. He had stiff, hair-like bristles at the base of his bill called rictal bristles. Then there were birds that belied their names like the White-browed Scrub Robin which looked more like a large wren. Indigo Birds, a black bunting-like species, came to join the Red-billed Quelea and the orange and black Northern Red Bishop birds in large flocks on the ground, scratching out seeds and finding nesting material now that the rains were coming. One particularly interesting bird was the Black-throated Honeyguide. Honeyguides are often mentioned in books about Africa. I couldn't imagine any honey at Gahla but now that the bushes were blooming, the insects could be expected to appear. This species was indeed the one that had been known to lead humans to honey but it is not the honey that appeals to the bird. It is the wax which they eat—along with the bee.

I was finishing with Ayub and Aden by the last week of July. Ayub had tried my patience as he wanted to prove that he was bright enough to learn the technical work, a fact that I had never doubted, but he thought manual chores were beneath him and balked at staining and weighing. I also felt that he already had a career as an interpreter, unlike the other boys who wanted desperately to learn something as a way to better themselves and their families. Though I knew it was almost impossible that they would get work in a lab in Addis, where knowledge of Amharic and/or English was imperative, I hoped that perhaps they could get work in Djibouti or some rural clinic if such a thing ever came to be. They were already proficient at their present clinic duties and knowledge of basic lab technique might benefit them in the health care field.

My heat rash had spread even to my upper arms, where the Afar people noticed it and were concerned. Vinod had given me antihistamines but they only helped if I took so much that I was weaving on my lab stool. Some of that dizziness might have been from dehydration. Vinod had doubts about the idea of giving me rehydration salts to drink. We had no way to test for electrolytes in the blood and he felt that overdosing was too likely. He wanted me to put more salt on my food but my stomach seemed to accept food only early in the day. I had used my pretty *natala* as a sheet for my mattress to avoid contact with the plastic and attempted to keep my skin dry. This proved to be an impossible task since we were drenched in sweat most of the day and night. One afternoon, itching all over my upper body, I asked Vinod if there was something more we could do. Vinod said that he could start me on prednisone. I hesitated as prednisone is well known for affecting electrolytes. I asked him whether he thought that was a good idea. He said, "I think you should go home." It was an idea that I had already faced. I had not weighed myself but I had to tie my pants up with a cord in the morning. Otherwise they wouldn't stay up. I had intended to go the whole six months but to stay and get sicker was not smart. I had been in mission almost two months. I thought I could last one more.

The next day I told Maria that I would go home at the first of September. She understood completely. She said that she often had felt sorry for me, especially as I sat in the sun at the microscope. I was surprised at the sentiment. I felt that I had it easier than others in mission. The doctors and nurses had longer hours and more confusion in which to work. Staff members and aides were constantly in and out of the clinic area, fetching supplies and asking questions while the medical staff was trying to examine and diagnose. They were faced with an inability to communicate without the interpreters who were not always available as well as a never ending phalanx of sick people waiting. We all underwent some hardship but I worked in a relatively clean and quiet lab with adequate supplies. When I was a child, I was discouraged from saying "I can't." My grandmother could be depended on to tell me "You can do it. Our people were pioneers." I did not feel like a proper pioneer.

The Afar had Their Own Heroes

One morning as I looked out the lab window I saw people running toward a pile of mats. There was an obvious emergency. Vinod was on his way back from Addis and Maria and Jose had just left for their break, so only the Afar staff was in the clinic. I ran out and had to elbow myself through the crowd, not understanding what had happened. Hiyu was already there and told me that the deboiter had fallen with a little girl inside. The men quickly cleared away the debris. The child was alive but dazed. The men carried her back to the clinic, where Kadir examined her and pronounced her well. I was impressed with the skills of our Afar medics. Hiyu had done a great job of crowd control. Kadir, like the other Afar nurses that I met, was used to working on his own. Nurses there are not supervised and obliged to wait on doctor's orders as they are in the United States. They are more like Advanced Nurse Practitioners or Physician's Assistants. Hassan and Kadir could have functioned in a clinic setting without us, had there been a clinic in which to work and any money with which to pay them.

Vinod was not happy to be back in mission. He confided that he didn't see how he could do three more months but neither would he hear of leaving early. We agreed that the illness and the fatigue were taxing but it was the isolation that made it hard. We now had an Afar Sheik in mission. His name was Sheik Ahmed and he was in his sixties, a respected religious leader, very approachable with excellent English. Already, he had come to the lab to help me with questions the trainees needed answered and proved to be a tremendous asset. He came to be a liaison with our patients but had already voiced the opinion that we, the expat staff, had to get away from mission and from work, at least occasionally

With more patients I was doing more kinds of tests. Though we were primarily a TB clinic, the Afar people had nowhere else to go and came to us with all sorts of illnesses. I was asked to look at a direct smear from a young dysentery patient. For the first time in my life I saw a motile amoeba in a stool sample. Inching along in the microscope field

was an Entamoeba histolytica with the peculiar unidirectional movement described in every textbook but which no tech I ever knew had
actually seen. We almost always had to rely on the characteristics of
the passive cysts to identify this parasite and I had found the cysts only
once in the States. Diarrhea is particularly dangerous in a child and can
kill within days. Fortunately we had a good supply of Metronidazole.

As we were growing and using up our stock, Maria informed me
that we needed to order supplies. Since I had an inventory of the supplies we had at the opening of the lab, it was a fairly simple matter
to determine how much stain we had used: cotton, slides, cups, etc.,

but our test volume had greatly increased. With the help of Vinod and Maria, I upped my estimate to allow for the new patient load. It was strange to think that, with the distance these supplies would have to travel, from Paris in some instances, another tech would unload these supplies after I was gone. It had been my lab from day one and now the lab would belong to someone else. I had faith by this time, though, that the new tech would be competent. The organization of the inventory, the quality of my team, the involvement of the people in MSF, assured me that healing would go on.

Weapons Sales — A Far Cry from Aid

A delegation of the Ethiopian government came to mission one day in July. The administration of Ethiopia is divided into nine ethnically based regions with two governing centers in Addis and in Dire Dawa. The delegation head was the representative for the Afar tribal area. The visit was quite a spectacle as the Minister representing the Afar was accompanied by bodyguards who carried Kalashnikovs. No guns had been allowed in mission, a rule that had been rigidly enforced when patient families came armed and the picture symbol, a rifle with a red bar through it, was posted on all MSF vehicles. This prohibition had been hard won as guns are much a part of the culture. In fact, if you look up the term "Afar Warrior" on the Internet you are sure to find a picture of a young Afar with his Kalashnikov propped high on his shoulders behind his neck, a hand balancing each end. It was only the need for medical care and the opportunity to earn some money that had made it possible for us to stay gun free.

Per UNICEF, that Kalashnikov, known in the US as the AK47, can be bought for as little as the price of a chicken in Uganda or a bag of maize in Mozambique. The UNICEF website states, "Small arms and light weapons are involved in internal conflicts, crime and violence" and lead to the "militarization of society." So where do the rifles and other weapons come from? Between 2005 and 2008, the US sold $18 million worth of weapons of different kinds to Djibouti and $12 million to Ethiopia. In 2006 over $25 million went to the Horn of Africa in direct arms purchases from the United States. William Church writes on www.americanchronicle.com that private arms sales have also skyrocketed. The US Defense Dept. estimates that $9.5 million in private arms sales occurred in 2005. Nine million dollars' worth of those arms went to Uganda. The US is by far the largest exporter of all arms at 41% of the world's total arms deliveries in 2009, according to the Congressional Research Service report. Russia, in second place, barely delivers one-fourth the amount at 10.6%. Germany and the UK are next followed by China, all in the single digit percentages. Israel is a rising star in the arms trade and it was an Israeli, Hamoch Miller, reportedly partnered with an American retired military officer, who was indicted this year for illegally selling hundreds of AK47s to Somalia though there has been an arms embargo on Somalia since 1992. About the arms embargo, Hervé Couturier writes of the UN report, "the sixteen year embargo has been constantly violated with weapons coming from Yemen and financed by Eritrea as well as Arab and Israeli donors." "The illegal trafficking is fueling the bloody conflict in the Horn of Africa... and is aiding rampant piracy off the Somali coast." Arms smuggled to Somalia are bound to impact the Afar area since Somalia is separated from the region only by small Djibouti, which the Afar transit regularly.

The US is not blameless in the civil war still going on in Somalia. According to the group Foreign Policy in Focus, both the USSR and the US wanted control of Somalia during the Cold War because of its location on oil routes from the Persian Gulf. During the 1980s we sent more than $200 million in aid to Somalia, enough to make it dependent, then pulled out in 1991, leaving Somalia in a "failed state" status. Tom Ofansky in an interview for Frontline (Feb. 2002), describes Afghanistan as a failed state, used to train and hide people, and Somalia as a failed state in anarchy. He says, "In Somalia, you have a group there known as al-Itihaad, which supposedly is a terrorist group. But one of the things it has done is provide stability in certain areas, through the establishment of Islamic courts; they've run health clinics; they've run schools. They're providing services no one else can provide. And, I think, when groups like that start getting the support of local communities, that's when you can enter into a breeding ground for trouble."

It is obvious that the arms we sell to supposedly friendly nations do not stay put. The military in Afghanistan is now giving M-16s to Afghan troops instead of AK47s, partly so they can tell if the arms are winding up in the hands of the Taliban. The rifles we saw all over Ethiopia could have come from anywhere. Herbert Ekwe-Ekwe, Professor of History and Politics and Director of the Center for Cross-Cultural Studies in Dakar, feels that arms sales to Africa are precipitating and exacerbating many of Africa's problems. On opendemocracy.net, June 15, 2005, an excerpt is posted by Professor Ekwe-Ekwe, entitled, "Ban Arms Sales to Africa, Nothing Else Needed." He says, "That Africa is poor is an assumption share by the G8s. It is also false: Africa remains one of the world's most richly endowed continents, with an immense human and non-human resource base to feed, clothe, house, educate, provide peace and security and construct an advanced civilization for its peoples. But to achieve this, Africans must dismantle their 'inherited' genocide-states through which ruthless African regimes have murdered 15 million of their peoples in the past four decades. This... is the emergency that threatens Africa's very survival." He continues to assert that Western governments are not really trying to reverse the "stupendous inflow of capital from Africa." That inflow would include payment for arms. He says, "The governments and institutions that have taken a long time to establish control and exploitation of Africa will not quickly abandon their spoils." Meanwhile, in Ethiopia and elsewhere, the rifles proliferate faster than the sandgrouse.

It was decided that the official's bodyguards would be allowed to keep their weapons as it was feared that we would be held responsible if something should happen to the Minister while on MSF premises. Though the bodyguards were big men, the Minister himself was a slight man in keeping with his Afar heritage. He was very formal and he walked with what I can only describe as a subdued swagger. He announced that he wished to have a discussion and just the process of arranging the talk became an undertaking. Finally, there was a meeting of all the expat staff and the Afar medics, with the Minister and his retinue, all of us formed a crowded circle in the dining hut. It was an extended interchange. First the Minister would speak in Afaraf. This would then be translated into French. I'm not sure why, because those such as Hassan who did not speak enough English did speak Afaraf. Then the same words would be translated into English. It was surprising to me that the Minister did not speak English as the previous official had spoken it well, but we all exercised our patience and it finally was clear to everyone what request was being made.

The Ethiopian government wanted MSF to take over the Dubti hospital. The members of the expat staff exchanged glances. We had known for some time that supplies were short at the hospital and MSF had helped with the shortages, but the attitude of the medical staff at Dubti was a problem in itself. The midwife, Anne-Marie, now planned to go home as she was not being given work by the native doctors on staff in the hospital. Expat surgeons who had tried to demonstrate new techniques and treatments had not had much following. It sounded to me like a contest of egos, with no winners. The word within our group had been that MSF planned to pull out of Dubti altogether. Maria told the minister that we would have to contact Addis, who would then contact Paris, as it was not a decision that could be made by us. The minister was satisfied with that. He did briefly visit the infirmary and tents and was wandering around by himself in the courtyard when I returned from the lab in the late afternoon. Much to my surprise, he called to me by name. I went over and he told me in perfectly good English how much his people appreciated having me come to their country and operate the lab for them. I made an effort to be gracious in my turn but I couldn't help thinking how much quicker the meeting could have been if it had been conducted in only a couple of languages. I suppose it was important for him to speak in Afaraf, given his position as the representative for that group. He probably spoke French, also, so he sat through hearing the same explanations and pleasantries three times. It was my first experience in diplomacy. I knew I would never have the patience to do it routinely.

Parasites and Playacting

During the first week of August, I felt sick one morning and had to go outside, where I threw up the Larium which I had just taken and which I knew I would have to retake, a waste of meds. I was too tired and weak to work and was obliged to return to my shelter and lie down. I awoke to find both Vinod and Maria crouched over me. Vinod had juiced oranges and added sugar to revive me. He admitted that he was suffering from the same malaise and from exhaustion. Jose had been sick, too, for several days, and was talking about stopping mission. His complexion was gray. Maria, despite her definitive diagnosis of Giardia, was holding her own.

One evening after dinner, a worker came to tell Vinod that one of the TB patients who had completed her treatment in the hospital and been released to continue as an outpatient was very sick. She had been coming to the DOTS tent daily for her meds but had not mentioned her illness. When Vinod got to her deboiter it was suspected and later confirmed that she had malaria. She was transferred to a hospital tent and IV's started but the prognosis was not good. She was young, pretty and had responded to the TB treatment so well. It felt like one step forward and two steps back.

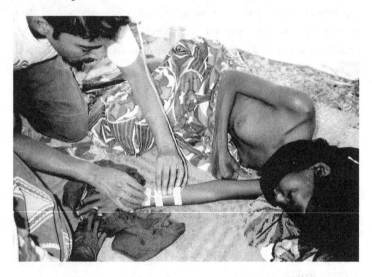

In the lab, I was attempting to teach Hammadou and Adais to take their training further. Vinod did not think they would ever be adequate to staff a lab on their own, which was certainly true but I hoped to teach them the manual skills which would allow them to assist a tech. I could not keep both boys indefinitely as they were needed in the hospital tents and clinic, and I needed to get one more young man trained before I left, but I hope they were able to use the skills they picked up at some time in their future.

We practiced sticking each other's fingers in order to learn to make blood smears and to dilute white cell counts using the special pipette and diluting fluid, then loading the White Cell Counting Chamber. I showed them the grid of the prepared counting chamber under the scope so they would know what a properly loaded chamber should look like. We still had no common language so I had to resort to play acting to get the idea across that we were pretending to be patients. One day I had pricked Adais' finger and, after some coaching, he had pricked mine, but I didn't think they understood that we were practicing methods to use on patients. So I used one of the clean rags we kept for cleaning and draped it over Hammadou's head. I told them that he was now Fatima, a common name for female patients since Fatima was Mohammed's daughter. They giggled and snickered as boys anywhere would do, but were not in the least insulted. Hammadou rearranged the head covering to a more realistic drape and stuck out his finger so that I knew he did get the idea. I got another laugh from them when I got out my new plastic fly swatter that I had proudly obtained in Addis. Both boys thought it was very funny to watch me chase flies around the lab, trying to kill them, and they laughed especially hard when I missed. I had seen quite elaborate fly flicks in Addis made of long combed horse hair but they looked like they would just brush the flies aside, not kill them. I had bought, instead, the usual flat plastic swatter, probably made in China. Thinking I would show my amused assistants that it wasn't as easy as it looked, I offered them the swatter. They both refused. I believe it was out of respect for the flies, another form of wildlife.

The boys probably did not have any idea that the flies would carry disease organisms on their legs. I didn't expect the boys to swat flies but I did feel that fly patrol needed explaining, along with other things that they might not understand. When he had time, I asked Sheik Ahmed to come up and interpret. Some things even he could not convey in the Afar tongue. For instance, I thought we should discuss AIDS. The boys had learned about its transmission in their training but I learned that there was no Afar word for virus, though they did have a word for bacteria.

We received word that a tech would come from France the first week of September, but Maria was arranging to get a tech from Addis just in case the expat tech was late or decided not to stay. Though I was still unwell, I felt that I should stay until the expat tech came on board to show her the routine, but Maria said that I could meet her in Paris and explain then. I had typed up all my procedures and posted them at the appropriate benches for reference, but I printed out some copies to take to her. I had no way of knowing how well she read English but the lab manual which I had been given was all in French and as I had been able to puzzle some things out, I hoped that she could get something out of my effort to make her life easier.

I knew Maria and Vinod were concerned about me. The joint pain waxed and waned but was never absent, and I was very tired. I would go to bed at about 8 PM every night and fall immediately asleep, not waking even during the torrential rains and accompanying fierce winds that often swept over us during the night. I thought it rained hard in Florida, but these rains would be so sudden and abundant that the water had no time to run off or soak in and instead streaked across the gray earth in sheets and stood in puddles on the porous sand.

Chapter 8. Further Into the Inferno: A Geological Laboratory

Though he knew we should see something more of Ethiopia, Vinod resisted going away for even a day. He was operating on auto-pilot and it took the coaxing of Sheik Ahmed to convince him to take one day off and to accompany us to the thermal springs and salt lakes of the far eastern section of the Afar Triangle. On the journey were my trainee Adais, our native nurse Hassan, our regular driver Ali, Sheik Ahmed, Maria, Vinod and myself. We started out early on the morning of August 10, rattling around in the back of a beat up Land Cruiser with Sheik Ahmed and the driver up front and the rest of us arranged on the two side benches in the back or, in the case of Adais, on the floor. Maria had understood that we would be going swimming, an idea I could hardly credit, but she had her bathing suit ready.

The drive took several hours and there was too much creaking noise for talking, but I was entertained by looking for birds and other wildlife. I was able to point out two kinds of antelope and some baboons that the others didn't immediately see. (In this instance, the habit was a positive. It was not a positive at home when, driving a car, I often overshot my turn or took the wrong one because my attention was on a bird or some wildflower.) My persistence paid off on the road to the salt lakes when I spotted an Eastern Pale Chanting Goshawk. By that time, I had pored over my Kenyan bird book until I could ID some new birds pretty quickly, which was fortunate, as a quick look was all I got of this pearl gray bird of prey with black wing tips.

As the land began to get wetter, I got one more new species, the Desert Cisticola, a bird grouped in the family of warblers. It has a warbler bill but the muted streaked plumage of a sparrow. Despite its name, the Desert Cisticola is usually found near water and soon after we saw it, we did come to the first of the hot springs.

Maria found a hut in which to change and donned her bathing suit in preparation for a dip. I had not even considered bringing a bathing suit to mission so I just prepared to go in wearing my dress with the printed sea horses which my daughter had bought me on a Caribbean island and which was still bright despite many rubbings on the wash board by Aisha or Saida.

Water anywhere attracts insects and thus birds, so I was surprised to find two old friends near the hot springs, the Barn Swallow, flashing blue and russet above me and the Glossy Ibis. The Glossy is not as widespread as the White Ibis and is more beautiful, being one of those birds that can only be appreciated with binoculars so as to fully visualize the purple, green and burgundy sheen of the feathers.

It must have been a pretty big surprise to Maria when she saw the steam rising from the spring. I put my hand in and very quickly pulled it back. The water was not far from boiling. We moved farther from the vent to a shallower part of the pool, which was cooler though not nearly cool enough for immersion. Getting in the spirit, though, our Afar companions stripped down to their underwear and splashed the water across their legs and chests. None of the men seemed aghast at the sight of Maria in her bathing suit, a conservative one-piece, and neither did they stare. They were also not embarrassed at being seen in their boxers. I believe this was partly because that they did not judge us by the standards they used for their own women and partly because they viewed this as a getaway day, a day to relax and have fun.

While they were splashing, I was training my binoculars on the lakes in the distance, a chain of them stretching away to the horizon and across the border into Djibouti. I understood Sheik Ahmed to say we were looking at Dubi Lake but my research has not found that name listed among the lakes in the chain. I may have misheard him or Dubi could be a local name. From the location I assume that we were gazing from a distance over the chain of six Ethiopian Rift Valley lakes that culminate in Lake Abbe, which used to be called Lake Abhebad. We could not see that lake to find out whether it does indeed have the blue-green water that is evident on satellite maps or whether it is, as the name implies, "white water." Had we been able to travel further, we might have seen the limestone chimneys and the many colors associated with mineral deposits in those thermal areas. Where we were, the land was, as Wilfred Thesiger, a 1933 explorer, described it, "country as dead as a lunar landscape" (*Africa's Rift Valley*, Colin Willock and the editors of Time-Life Books).

Thesinger was looking for the mouth of the Awash River and he didn't believe the Afar tribesmen who assured him that there was no outlet from the river to the sea. It took him several days and a long hot trudge to convince himself that the river dead ended in these mostly saline lakes eighty miles from the Red Sea. The thermal activity results from the fact that the area straddles the juncture of three tectonic plates. It is one of the few places on earth where continental drift can be observed on dry land. According to the website of NASA's earth observatory, the African plate splits into the Nubian and Somalian plates in the Afar Triple Junction located in the middle of the Afar Depression. It is described as the "birthing ground of a new ocean" (*Oceanography, An Introduction*, Ingmanson and Wallace, Wallace Publishing 1973). The margin of a tectonic plate runs right up the center of the Red Sea and the Gulf of Aden, and the southern part of the Red Sea appears to have been formed by rifting between Africa and Arabia. Theoretically, by the same process, the Indian Ocean will one day flood the low-lying Afar triangle and a new sea will be born. Some sources are already calling it the Afar Sea.

The area is reminiscent of Yellowstone Basin with its steam vents and hot pools. *Ethiopia*, a tourist booklet produced by the Ethiopian Tourist Commission, describes the Rift as a "giant tear across the earth's surface, visible even from space." It crosses Ethiopia from northwest to southeast and, though it results in desert in the northeast, in the southwest there are indeed lakes that are appropriate for bathing. Perhaps Maria had heard of those lakes but anyone who tried to bathe in our hot spring would have come out parboiled rather than refreshed. This little spring was a relief valve for the molten material upwelling beneath. Indeed the active volcano, Erta Ale, also called Dama Ale, lies next to Lake Abbe on the Ethiopian/Djibouti border directly east of where we splashed hot water on ourselves. My photo of the day shows a wadi or wetland stretching away to the horizon, shrouded in mist or steam, with a conical shaped mountain on the left in the distance.

I had no chance to see the flamingos for which Lake Abbe is famous in birding circles, but my searching did turn up a Pink-backed Pelican, very like our White Pelicans, which are also found in the area, but smaller and giving the impression of going bald. The feathers on the backs of the birds I saw were so scant that their pink skin showed through.

Sheik Ahmed told us about the practice of salt gathering by the Afar for centuries in this mineral rich area. Salt collects around the saline lakes as it does in the Bonneville Salt Flats in Utah. Salt was and is used by the Afar as currency in trade for commodities they wish to buy. In *Africa's Rift Valley*, as late as 1974 the author describes meeting this "specialized breed of Afar" who were "levering the salt from the lake and chipping it with hand tools into rectangular bars....Then the camel trains carry the salt bars to market." Mr. Willock describes the group of salt mining Afar as "industrious and peaceful." It seems to me that this back-breaking work in temperatures as high as 135 degrees Fahrenheit would leave absolutely no energy for anything but peace. Furthermore, those Afar presumably did not see the explorers as a threat to their livelihood. Our Afar in Gahla were not digging salt. There was money to be made in mission, but the Afar in the north are still taking their salt to the border with the highlands and trading it for needed supplies, and if need be they would probably still defend that resource with the ferocity for which they are known.

Blissfully Ignorant

Due to the length of time it would take us to return to mission, we were soon obliged to leave our hot pool and start the journey home. We stopped in a village for lunch. The restaurant was shaded and cool inside compared to the desert heat. A waitress came around with a pitcher of water. The water is poured over the hands before eating. Though at first I didn't understand the custom, it soon made sense, as we all ate from the same platter, scooping up the rice and bits of meat with our hands. It is customary to use the right hand only. The meal was as good to us as a fine restaurant dinner in our home countries. Just to have meat was a treat, and to eat at a table was really "uptown." We had lost the concept of fun, immersed as we were in our demanding work in an isolated existence, but we found it again that day under the white hot sun in a dusty village on the edge of a "lunar landscape."

On the way back to mission we saw a jackal and a Soemmerring's Gazelle, a graceful animal with black lines in the face. Though they are supposed to be widespread and were often heard, I never saw a jackal at mission. They do not live in close packs like wild dogs but rather singly or as a pair, mated for life. The mother jackal moves her litter to a new den often so she is not likely to be found. They did not have anything to fear from the natives. People might have been at risk of attack by the Afar but the wildlife was never molested.

I was happy that day to be away from mission for a short break with friends, seeing new sights and new birds, blissfully unaware that a few years later in September and October 2005, earthquakes of magnitudes up to 5.6 (according to the USGS) would rend the Depression as they had many times before and a volcano would erupt. It created a "fissure more than 500 meters long and about 60 meters deep," according to the website of The Global Volcanism Program. From the map on the same website, I know the erupting volcano was west of the area we visited, but similar conditions exist where we stood that day and a thermal release could easily have hissed up from the pressure cooker right while we were there in August 2001.

When we returned to Gahla, we learned that our young TB/malaria patient had died of cerebral malaria. She had become comatose and had stopped putting out urine. Kadir had done all that could be done for her but Vinod suffered at her death. He blamed himself for leaving for the day, though we all knew that she had simply waited too long to seek treatment. Once malaria reaches a certain stage, nothing can stop the inevitable. He then chided himself for not noticing her condition when she came to the DOTs tent. It was not justified, as Vinod was now the sole doctor for a community of over two hundred souls, the vast majority of whom were sick with at least one life threatening illness. Maria and I reminded him that he probably didn't even see the woman when she came for her drugs as he was seldom the one manning the DOTS tent. He rallied, as he had to do, but it was obvious that he was tired.

Maria had arranged for a cement trough to be installed under one of the tents. It is important to Muslims to wash their dead and it had been difficult to keep the bodies clean when the loved ones tried to wash them on the ground. This patient had the dubious honor of being the first to use the trough. Her people laid her to rest in the burial ground beyond the settlement. I wondered how full that space would be before I went home.

CHAPTER 9. THE AFAR

The Afar tribe is not named after the Afar triangle which forms their homeland. It is the other way round. The Danakil Depression is called the Afar Triangle in honor of this tough people that are almost its only denizens. The Triangle comprises 58,000 square miles between the Red Sea and the Gulf of Oman at roughly 11.75 N latitude and 40.95 E longitude. It is unarguably one of the hottest places on earth. According to the World Wildlife Fund, the human population is "less than ten persons per kilometer and in some areas less than one person per kilometer," with the "dominant ethnic groups being the nomadic pastoralists, the Afar, and a Somali clan, the Issas."

I learned about the Issa fairly early in my mission as Fred told us that some of the Afar men from the crew building the living quarters had asked for time off to "go kill some Issa." The Afar believed that members of the Issa tribe had stolen some camels. This was before Sheik Ahmed came to bridge the cultural divide and, since it did not immediately concern our mission, Fred was told to tell them that they could "have time off but NOT for the purpose of killing Issas." We never heard, but I think it unlikely that any Issa were killed in the incident, especially since it was explained to the men that they would lose wages for every day they took off. I did see a small family of Issa near the road when traveling from mission to Addis. The family still wore the brown clothing (like sacking material) that I was told used to be the apparel of the Afar, too. Like so many feuds, it was hard to know whether there were indeed new infringements at the time or whether it was a self-perpetuating conflict. We had one Somali in camp who was helping with the building of the permanent housing. He looked very like the Afar to me and was well accepted by the rest of the staff. I believe that the Afar and the Issa must have come from the same stock as there is no natural boundary between the countries. Somalia takes up where Ethiopia leaves off, the two of them with Eritrea and little Djibouti forming the horn of Africa.

The Travel Channel did a special a few years ago (a little sensationalized), showcasing the Afar, called "the Last Warriors." In the film, Ethiopian cattle were pictured and reported to be used as currency. I can say that in Gahla, goats were the staple for milk and meat, and camels ruled. One day a camel was butchered and it was cause for celebration. Fred took a picture of the beast after the throat had been cut with the razor sharp jile. The men took pride in the process and everyone was excited about sharing the meat. The Afar diet, almost totally comprised of milk, their coarse bread and a little goat meat, must have benefitted from any addition.

The children in mission were a joy to all of us. Unlike the adults, they showed no reserve. One little girl named Hawie, probably short for Hawah, would sneak through the gap between fence and gate, her light boned little body slipping easily in and out at will. She was a beautiful child who always wore a necklace of beads around her neck. She liked to sit with us and became a special pet. I had brought some tissue paper in different colors and cellophane tape from home and showed a few of the kids how to make paper "flowers." I'm not sure that they even understood what a flower was, but they liked the activity.

I was a diversion and soon had a retinue of children following me around. If I asked to take their picture, the boys would stand up straight and the little girls would giggle and quickly find something to cover their heads if possible, playing grown-up lady. We often saw kids dressed in clothes which must have come from some relief agency or have been bought third hand at a bazaar. I have a picture of a boy about six years old wearing a girl's dress complete with puffed sleeves and eyelet edged collar. The Afar babies did not wear diapers. They just went around bare bottomed and squatted at will. It certainly saved a lot of diaper changing.

One afternoon a group of children came up to the lab carrying a bowl of camel's milk and offered it to me as a gift. I was well aware that the unpasteurized milk of the camels or goats could carry mycobacteria. Even elephants have been known to catch TB in captivity, but I could not bring myself to refuse such a precious commodity. I sipped it and they were satisfied. It had a strong taste. I later took the remainder down to the kitchen and the kitchen girls were thrilled to get it.

It is difficult to get to know anyone well if you don't share a common language. I saw Hassan, our native nurse, often and he would always nod and ask after my welfare, if there was someone to interpret, but I could not converse with him. Hassan took a very tough line with his fellow Afar, using the megaphone to yell Hitleresque exhortations at them about infractions such as spitting on the ground without covering it afterward or defecating close to camp. He used vehement hand motions when taking anyone to task, and the tone of voice did not need interpreting. I asked Milton once whether this kind of approach was necessary and he backed Hassan up, repeating the idea that the Afar respect force. Hassan had certainly accomplished much. He appeared to be in charge of the local Afar Pastoralist Development Association, a group that, as of 2009, numbered over 750 workers. The APDA does much more than train the healthcare workers who were staining in my lab. The group was begun by Australian nurse, Valerie Browning and her husband, Ismael Ali Gardo. As will be seen later in this book, they have taken on responsibility for road building and for rainwater catchment devices that will help to assure water resources during droughts. They practice veterinary skills, treating and vaccinating herd animals. Since 2004, the regional bureau of education adopted the program that the APDA initiated of operating mobile schools, following the nomads as they travel in order to bring education to them. The program goes beyond training literacy teachers. According to their website, they are also involved in "training women extension workers to bring about more involvement of women in the community and to end the unsafe practices of female genital mutilation and forced marriage."

I believe that Hassan cared deeply for his tribe. It may be that he felt he needed drama to motivate or discipline the undereducated Afar. I never saw him berate or harshly criticize the APDA boys who were already working in the clinic.

Kadir, the other native nurse, was very different both in personality and in appearance. He was a big man, but gentle, and handsome by anyone's standards. His skin was dark and his face square. I always thought he looked more Amhar than Afar, while Hassan, with his narrow face and male pattern baldness, looked very like his countrymen. Perhaps some of the difference was due to age, as Hassan was middle aged while Kadir did not look more than thirty. The difference may also have been an indication that the Afar culture was evolving, perhaps rapidly. John Hooker of the Carnegie Mellon University wrote an abstract in which he maintains that a machismo attitude comes of living with violence and danger. Perhaps, jobs to sustain them and a place to live that is not a continual struggle and which they do not have to continually defend would pacify the Afar men over time.

The kitchen girls became very familiar. The two whom I got to know, Aisha and Saida, did a lot of the cooking while "Hamadini," the cook, provided the expertise. That was a nickname he got from his preference for cooking Italian food. Having first worked in an Italian household, I think that was the only cooking he knew. Only twice did he cook anything that was not pasta or rice. One of those dishes was *ful*, a mixture of cooked fava beans, onion and garlic with olive oil poured over all. Ful is the Egyptian word for fava beans. It was eaten at breakfast Most of the staff liked ful, which is popular in Egypt and it added some protein to our diet.

The other dish was cooked on a special night. Aisha had noticed how little meat was served. The Afar women can own their own sheep and goats and make their own decisions about how to sell them. This small girl had a sheep and a goat butchered from her own herd to be fed to us. Hamadini outdid himself that night. The lamb was cooked over a fire, moist and tender, with what I think were sesame seeds encrusting it. The goat, too, was good and very much appreciated. Sometimes the Afar could be recalcitrant and ornery, but then there were acts such as Aisha's.

Afar Origin and Practice

The Afar speak a Cushitic language. This differs from the Semitic languages; it did not originate in the Arabian regions. Amharic, the language spoken in Addis, is a Semitic language. This fact surprised me as the Afars, to me, have a more Arabic appearance than do the Amhars and the Afars claim to be descended from the Arabs. The term Danakil first appears in the writing of thirteenth century Arab geographers. Cushitic language speakers are believed to be the original inhabitants of Ethiopia. Cushites of one kind or another lived in the region during the second millennium BC and had close associations with Egypt; Cushites are mentioned in the Bible. The Somali and some Oromo are also Cushites. According to tradition, Menelik I, the son of Solomon and the queen of Sheba, founded the first kingdom of Ethiopia, called Abyssinia in those days, in the northern part of the country. History can document the kingdom of Aksum, extending from before the time of Christ to about AD 700. Ethiopian Christianity began in the Aksumite kingdom but when Islam came to Ethiopia in about AD 600 the lowland people were gradually converted to the new religion and Aksum lost power. These lowland people included the Afar.

Sheik Ahmed often sat with me on the mat after I had taken my bucket shower in the evening before dinner. It was a good opportunity for me to learn about his culture. One night I asked him about the kind of religion the Afar practiced. He replied, "They are Sufi Muslims." This was a new kind of Muslim to me; my reading has revealed that the Sufis are a mystical subgroup of the Sunni faith. The whirling dervishes of Turkey are Sufi Muslims. The Afar do not whirl, to my knowledge, but several sources mention that there are vestiges of the old pagan religion in the Afar practices. I did not recognize any shrines but I did notice the Afar reluctance to kill wild creatures. This may have been due to the animalistic nature of the old religion, a desire to live in harmony with them. Some sources give this reluctance to take game as the reason for the continued existence of the region's wildlife, including the threatened Wild Ass.

As for practice, I saw both men and women bowing in prayer to the east, using a cloth or mat beneath them and chanting, but I think much of the behavior that we saw was cultural, not religious. I saw one old woman demonstrating the "ulu,lu,lu,lu,lu,lu" sounds that they make with their open mouths and tongues and use at times of excitement. It is often done at weddings and is demonstrated in the Travel Channel clip previously mentioned. It is sometimes done at births. A coordinator for Care, Intl., who was working with the Afar in 2007, was quoted in reference to the ululating. He said that, if a woman gives birth to a son, there is clapping and ululating. If she gives birth to a daughter, there is silence.

We sometimes saw activity from a distance and heard unfamiliar music made by primitive instruments in the village which had grown up around mission. I knew that the women were the musicians in the Afar clan and would like to have seen them play but, though we assumed some type of rite was being performed, we were not included in such private ceremonies.

One ritual could have been the circumcision of the boys which is portrayed, again sensationally, in "The Last Warriors." There is no specific age at which boys are circumcised but it is always done before marriage. Statistics show that 94% of Afar males are circumcised. Although female circumcision is a private matter, one girl at a time, male circumcision appears to be a rite of passage attended by the older males of the group, performed by an elder and celebrated by the clan. As you might imagine, it is not done under medical auspices but by traditional practitioners with no Novocain and an expectation that the boy will show the appropriate steel. I was told that circumcision for the boys is done only when food is plentiful so as to have enough for the feast, even if the rite has to be postponed for several years. It may have been that the money MSF was providing as wages to the workers made the ceremony possible.

From the interpreters, I learned that the Afar, as other Muslim faiths, can take up to four wives. Sheik Ahmed had only one wife and Kadir had divorced his wife. Ayub had two wives and the first wife visited him in Gahla. One of the national staff was courting a young woman whom it was rumored he would take as a second wife. The idea did not seem appropriate to Vinod and myself as we had met his first wife and she was said to be very upset about sharing her husband. We both knew, however, that it was one of those situations we had been warned was none of our business.

The national staff did try to inculcate the idea of family planning among the Afar. I am not sure how large the families were of Afar women in general as it was hard to tell parentage when so many were involved in a child's life. The grandmothers were ever-present and took over much of the childcare, even offering their sagging tits as pacifiers when the baby cried from hunger. The kids were truly, to quote Hillary Clinton, "raised by a village," so that just because the mother had only one or two children in the clinic, that didn't mean there weren't more children elsewhere. From different sources it can be estimated there were about four children per woman. Since a man could, however, have four wives if he could afford it, and if each wife had four children, that could multiply to sixteen children for one man. If the birth rate was not as high as might be expected, it was probably due to the ill health of many of the mothers. They were all anemic from the poor diet and the bleeding associated with being cut open for birth, sewn back up, rebroken, resewn, overworked and often diseased as well. Nature will preserve a mother's life at the expense of a fetus if the woman's health will not support both. Also, their practice of a form of endogamy, whereby every young son is expected to marry his maternal uncle's daughter, a first cousin, could only have multiplied the chances of genetic problems. Kadir told me that the response he often got to the mention of contraceptives was that the parents in question wanted to have "all the children that Allah would send them." His response to that was, "If Allah wanted you to have all these children, why isn't he sending you the food to feed them?"

It is impossible to read anything about the Afar without the mention of their trophy taking. Colin Willock, previously mentioned as the author of *Africa's Rift Valley*, says the Danakil in 1934 were still liable to "castrate and murder strangers to protect their scanty water supplies." Multiple sources tell of the old custom of hanging the dried scrota of their conquests around their waists and also of the requirement that an Afar boy must kill a man in order to be considered an adult. Sheik Ahmed assured me that these two customs were not now in force but the Afar in our camp were daily exposed to civilizing influences and not in need of water or food.

It is well documented that the Afar were involved in the East African slave trade, sometimes called the Islamic or Arab slave trade. In the West, we hear about the trade from West Africa as most of the slaves being shipped to the US and the islands came through the west coast of Africa, but a thriving trade existed for centuries that went east across Afar lands. Along that route would pass thousands of slaves from the south of Ethiopia and beyond, to be sold in Arab states. Though Mohammed decreed that masters should treat their slaves well, he did not specifically forbid slavery and economic factors resulted in the broadening of belief to include the idea that non-Muslims could be enslaved. The Ethiopian slaves, being mostly of the Oromo tribe, would cross the desert via camel trains to connect with the Gulf of Aden and the Indian

Ocean, where they were loaded on to ships bound for the Arab world. The death rate while passing through the Danakil was high from thirst and exhaustion. The Afar served as guides to Arab slave traders and called their route *adagagitta* (market route). The sultan of Assaita collected a tax from the slave merchants of Tigray and Wollo. According to "*Economics of the Indian Ocean Slave Trade in the Nineteenth Century*, groups of 30□50 Afar would move two hundred slaves at a time. The bulk of the slaves sent to Arab states were women to be used as concubines and domestic servants. Slaves were commonly kept in Ethiopia itself and slavery was not illegal until 1923, when the soon to be emperor Haile Selassie outlawed it in order to make Ethiopia acceptable for admission to the League of Nations. Estimates suggest that from one-half million to two and a half million Africans were collected from their villages to be sold as slaves in Arab countries during the nineteenth century. The website of Aden Airways, a subsidiary of British Airways, describes an encounter in 1888 in which the British warship H.M.S. Osprey came across Arab dhows carrying slaves in the Red Sea. They boarded the dhows and captured 213 victims from "Oromoland," only four of whom were men. The rest were women and children and were found to be in "pitiable condition." Considering the culture of the Afar in past years and their conviction that they are superior to other tribes, it is easy to believe that the Afar of old would improve their financial situation by trading in a people that they would consider to be of lesser value. And they were not, of course, the only group of people to benefit by the institution of slavery.

For myself, I can only report kindness and respect from the Afar. One morning, when we had had to stain more slides than usual, I got down to the dining room late and there was no more bread. Kadir overheard and sent someone to the restaurant in the nearest village to buy soft, white rolls for me. Another instance which stays with me is the evening I had to speak to my latest trainee after he had already gone home to his deboiter. I found our interpreter, Hiyu, who asked a lady nearby where the trainee might be found. She told him, and he then went into the mass of dwellings to fetch the boy. While I waited, the woman brought a stool for me to sit on and returned with "soup," a porridge the Afar had learned to make from MSF supplies, similar to

Cream of Wheat. She presented it to me with the utmost decorum and accompanying smile. We, in the West, would do well to take the time and effort to treat our fellows with the courtesy that is common in the Afar. Perhaps they are still ferocious with their perceived enemies but every member of their own tribe is valued, even temporary adoptees like me.

I asked Kadir about premarital sex among the Afar. He said it did occur, though it was discouraged. He went on to say that if a child resulted from one of these unions, it would be the property of the father. It appeared that the father made all the major decisions in an Afar child's life, and the fathers were not generally absentee dads. Fathers took an active role in caring for the children in hospital and it was often the father who stayed with a sick child and attended to his or her needs. The grandfathers also cared for children.

I wish that I had also asked Kadir about homosexuality among the Afar. It is officially condemned in the Muslim world but Muslims I have known have confided that it exists, though very much underground. It is illegal in Ethiopia altogether.

A Tribe Still in Battle

The 2007 census in Ethiopia showed 1,276,374 Afar in that country. Population estimates in Djibouti range from 130,000 to 170,000 with Eritrea adding another 300,000. In Djibouti they make up about one third of the population. That country was previously known as the French Territory of Afars and Issas.

Considering that there is a total population of 74 million people in Ethiopia, the slightly more than one million Afar are a very small minority, not large enough, apparently, to warrant much attention. We found the literacy rate to be about 2% in Gahla as opposed to a literacy rate of 42% in all of Ethiopia. As with all MSF missions, we wanted to improve the chances for these people to better themselves, so Maria arranged for a teacher to be hired. According to MSF rules we were not to use religious publications to teach and, at that time, the only book that had been translated into Afaraf was the Koran. The teacher had to come up with his own teaching materials, but we soon saw people going to class with pencil and tablet, women and children in particular.

It was vital that the women go, as a study published in *The Lancet* (Sept. 2010) reads, "for every one-year increase in the average education of reproductive age women, a country experienced a 9.5 percent decrease in child deaths." The study's co-author, Christopher J. L. Murray, explains that better educated woman are more likely to see the need for and to use disease prevention measures such as vaccines and mosquito nets. They are better able to understand germ theory and sanitation and, if a child does get sick, to take the child to the clinic early and to follow the treatment instructions. His study showed that increasing the gross domestic product of a nation does less to reduce child mortality than does improving education. We also hoped that the women would read the words of the Koran for themselves and come to question some of the misinterpretations that were affecting their lives.

It could be surmised that one reason the Afar do not get as much attention as they might from the national government is that they have chosen to maintain a distinct identity and have defended it mightily. The Afar have traditionally been led by sultanates within the Afar region. In 1975, the Afar revolted against the Derg after the Derg tried to arrest the sultan of Asayita. The sultan and his son escaped but Afar members of the group killed non-Afar in the area and burned property. They interfered with truck traffic, resulting in shortages in Addis. The Derg retaliated by killing many Afar, regardless of whether they were involved in the revolt or not. Great animosity followed and the Afar Liberation Front was formed. The Derg tried to absorb some Afar into the local administration in an effort to give them some regional control and avoid conflict, but not all Afar wanted to cooperate and two more political parties were formed. The Afar Liberation Front has since merged to some extent with the other two Afar-based parties to comprise a new party, the Afar National Democratic Movement. This Afar group holds eight seats in the national legislature out of a total of 526. Militant members of some groups still maintain their hope for Afar independence and it is rumored that the Afar Liberation Front is still alive. One thorn that pricks the Afar is the push westward by Amhara farmers, encroaching, in the opinion of the Afar, on their pastoral territory. Another encroachment involves the Issa Somalis. With their Somalia connections, they can obtain arms and they want to take over the better grazing territories in the Afar area. The flag associated with the Liberation Front consists of blue, white and green panels with crossed jiles in the center. It remains to be seen whether the traditional jile can compete with imported AK47s.

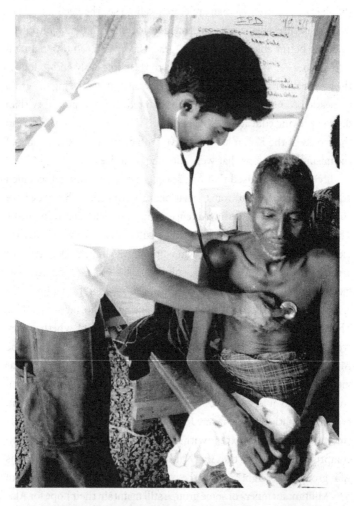

It is understandable why different sources list the Afar as descendants of either Egyptians or Arabs, given the centuries of nomadic life style. The tribe members in Gahla seemed to be bright and took to tasks willingly enough—if they were being paid—but they were not used to long hours and expected to break at 11AM no matter what work was waiting. It was always surprising to me that some of them could spend hours doing absolutely nothing and did not seem bored. That is probably my Westernized "fill every minute" view. Perhaps they were just too tired or unwell to do more than what is absolutely necessary, sapped by the climate, poor nutrition and ill health. They understood to some extent the transmission of disease but the native staff had to constantly remind them that spitting on the ground could spread what they called "the thin man's disease," a good moniker for TB as the fever and inflammation steal nutrition and strength, and the victims are often skin and bones. There is good reason for calling it "Consumption" in previous centuries.

The adult Afar could be entrenched in their ways. We all felt that the best chance for improvement in the lot of the Afar lay in the children. We tried to spend as much time with them as possible in the hope that in future they would not immediately treat every stranger with the animosity of the "Dreaded Danakil."

Chapter 10. A Question of Food

With the rains, the giant milkweeds bloomed. It was easy to recognize the genus as the leaves had the same milky sap and the flowers the same shape as the North American plants of the Asclepias genus; but these milkweeds reached above my head. The flowers were attractive to insects and birds. I got my first Variable Sunbird while he was inspecting the blooms. The Variable is small but has an iridescent throat and upper chest.

Our colony had grown by leaps and bounds. The nation of Ethiopia is broken up into state-type regions called wordas. We were in Welo Worda and I was now getting requisitions for patients from Tigray in the far north of the Afar territory. Word was spreading and people were coming long distances for treatment. Upwards of a hundred deboiters crouched around the hospital compound where only a few had stood when I came to mission. Afar women continued to be paid to build their traditional housing for recovering patients. I watched one young girl weaving the mats that we depended on for many purposes but which were most necessary in multiple thicknesses as roofs on the domed Afar houses. The new TB tent was even covered with an outside shelter of mats to keep it cool. The Afar girls must have been working overtime to make them.

Familiar faces had completed their time in hospital and now had moved to the family deboiter. We were trying to make sure we treated all contagious individuals since living in such close proximity was bound to spread the infection. I was on positive TB slide box number 3 and trainee number 5.

How to Feed the Multitudes

The gardener may have annihilated the flower seeds, but he did better with the watermelons. We had watermelon for dessert one night with the hope of other fresh fruits and vegetables to come. When the well had been dug so that we had plenty of water, some of our staff had demonstrated the foresight to plant food crops. I didn't see how the Afar could have much experience in gardening, nomads that they were, but Fred and Jose were giving advice and, if the pH of the soil didn't do them in, and they didn't get flooded, and if any one of a myriad of other disasters didn't befall them, it looked like there might be fresh beans for the new tech.

It has been suggested that genetically engineered crops may hold the key to better nutrition for Africa. Crops with genes that allow them to resist drought might help prevent famines, but they may not be widely available to African farmers. Though www.America.gov advertises genetically modified crops as a promising solution to food scarcity, Susan Sechler writes in *The American Prospect* (Winter 2002)[7] that "most biotech research is moving away from such public interest goals and toward private sector needs. In its aggressive push to protect intellectual property rights, the US government provides patents for new biotech crop varieties without regard to the importance of these crops to poor countries." Africa, along with Europe, originally feared GM crops. Peter Pringle, wrote in *So Shall We Reap* (Simon & Schuster, 2003)[8], about the Zambian government refusing corn from the US in 2002 because it contained genetically modified components though the Zambian people were starving. This decision was contrary in Western eyes but Mr. Pringle explains that the Zambian government feared that Zambian farmers would plant the whole kernel corn that they found among the aid grain and the resultant crops would lose their guaranteed GM free status, making them unsalable as exports to Europe.

Another type of genetic research uses a plant's own genes. Corn is said, in *So Shall We Reap* to have "self-help genes" that could be coerced into making the plant drought resistant. Richard Jefferson, in his Canberra, Australia nonprofit institute, is trying to use a combination

7 Reprinted in *World Hunger, op. cit.*
8 Reprinted in *World Hunger, op. cit.*

of plant breeding and genetic engineering by using genes from yeasts or bacteria to coerce a plant into making genes operational that are in place already but may only kick in at times of stress.

Conventional breeding has a place, too. Per the same article, Norman Borlaug, who has been called the father of the Green revolution in Mexico, cultivated ten new varieties of corn in developing countries, including Ethiopia, with a grant from the Carter Center. Borlaug claimed he could double or triple grain production in those countries within three years if public funds could be found. Therein lies another problem. More and more university professors sign exclusive deals with biotech companies in order to fund their research, genetic or otherwise. The resultant products cannot be used by anyone but the company who provided the funds. The Rockefeller Foundation has been trying to create a pool of biotech tools, genes and techniques, that could be used free of royalties by researchers engaged in work specifically by poor countries. While the debate continues about intellectual property rights, this patent impasse is not the primary problem to Norman Borlaug, who says that "there is already enough food in the world to keep people from starving. The solution is not to produce more food but to enable people to afford what is available."

Another part of the solution is population control. It is well known that the poorest mothers have the most children. This is not due to chance. A stressed oak tree will produce more acorns. There is a biological response to carry on the genes if the individual senses it will die. Poor women who are interviewed may want larger families than richer women, as security for their old age, but most do not want as many children as they have and no mother wants to see her child starve. A documentary concerning a family planning clinic in Kenya showed women lined up around the block to get contraceptives. It would be a worthwhile study to ascertain the growth in a given population when its children are fed and surviving versus the cycle of high birth rate, malnutrition and child mortality that is seen is the developing world today.

CHAPTER 11. CHRISTMAS

In August a surgeon came. He was headed for Dubti but paused at Gahla to bring us mail. All the packages that had accumulated must have put him over the weight limit and I was grateful. His name was Jean and he was a French-speaking Belgian. I took him up to the lab to show him our facility and when leaving, he pointed upward and called out, "Carmine Bee-eater." Another birder! What were the chances? When he found out I had a book, we had to go back to the lab and review my list, now grown to almost one hundred species.

That evening I sat in the dining room opening boxes. As Jean said, it was "like Christmas." My sister had sent fruit and nuts, coffee bags, books and colored pencils for the kids. In the box from home had come stickers and temporary tattoos. The kids were kept entertained for some time with those simple pleasures. I had come to know several names, little Hawi, Yasmin and Zafirah, Ali, Habbo and Daoud. The toddlers who could barely walk crawled around in the dirt with the slightly older siblings expected to watch them. My daughter sent sunglasses, insect repellent (non-greasy and enough to share), candy and crayons. My tech friends, Elaine and Judy, sent six rolls of duct tape and several cans of WD40, no doubt in response to having heard me say many times that there are two products necessary for human existence:

"for the living, Neosporin and for the non-living, WD40." As a medical unit we had the likes of Neosporin but not a drop of that irreplaceable Water Dispersant Experiment #40. Also in the box was a piece of paper dotted with a pattern for making a fan and a drink coaster from the bar where they were packing the box, having come in from an afternoon sail. It was good to laugh and feel the presence of such friends.

After dinner, I started passing around the goodies. My team was hesitant to take the food. "You should keep it," they said. There was no way I would hoard it, as I got as much good out of seeing them enjoy it as I did in eating it myself. Vinod took a small handful of M&Ms and passed the bag on. I had to keep insisting that they all take all they wanted and he finally broke down. "Pass me those M&Ms." Jose liked the dried fruit. After it had made its way around he said, "I could have, maybe, one more pesch (peach)?"

A friend from our Clearwater Quaker Meeting had sent a portable fan and batteries. The freight must have been exorbitant. We did have batteries in mission but the heat must have sapped them as they always seemed to be only half strength. These batteries were full of juice. I set that little fan up on the lab bench and my latest trainee and I enjoyed some moving air across our sweaty backs.

The next day I squirted the lock of the lab door with the magical WD40 and voilà! It no longer stuck. My trainee and I had been trapped in the lab one day because we couldn't get the door open and had to yell out the window until somebody heard us. It was a great relief not to fear closing the door. I gave the duct tape to Jose, who said "Thank you, thank you, thank you, merci, merci, merci." After having nothing but cellophane tape all these months, he was now supplied with something that would stick.

The next night was Jose's birthday. He had been depressed for some time, also sick in the generic way we were all sick. Maria wanted to make a cake for him. We didn't have any baking powder but I coerced the cook into making a round yeast bread and chopped up some of the dried fruit I had received from home to mix in. The oven was always problematic, hot on one side and hardly baking on the other but, such as it was, the "cake" was baked. We had no frosting but there was a little jam left over from the last trip to Addis so we frosted it with that. Then Maria brought out the pièce de resistance, a box of birthday candles, lovingly reserved from a trip to Addis. She and I crouched in the dining shelter with our backs to the wind trying to light the candles with eight members of the Afar staff peeking over our shoulders. They were unfamiliar with the custom and very curious. When Maria proudly presented Jose with his cake, we once again saw the big grin that had always been a part of him, a part that we had recently been missing. Eighteen people had a piece of cake that night. There were many grins.

My sister had sent some small Ziploc bags to facilitate sharing and my friend, Elaine, in a case of what must have been clairvoyance, had thrown in two self-sticking ribbon bows. Maria had mentioned that the next day would be her name day, a day the Greeks celebrate on the saint's day for whom they were named. I was able to make up two little bags of fruit and nuts, complete with a bow, for her and for Jose. They told me that no gift was ever sweeter. Jose, his English improving, told me that he had intended to make his fruit last, planning to eat just two pieces a day. He shook his head, though, and said, "First day, I take one piece, then one piece and one piece, then gone!"

Broadening Our Scope

We were seeing a bigger variety of patients. One was a man gored by a bull in the testicles. The scrotum was torn open and one testis was hanging by its stalk. Vinod went with him to the hospital in Dubti. We had been blessed by a second nurse, a French woman named Caren. She was sharing the shelter with Maria and me. The girl had carried with her a bottle of good French wine which we shared in honor of having her join us. She had an exciting initiation on her first day when a woman came in who had been in labor for many hours and needed a Caesarian. Many women who needed surgical intervention suffered greatly. Even if they were eventually able to deliver, the child was often stillborn. Due to the unrelenting pressure of extended labors, they were far too likely to develop a vaginal fistula; that is a tear between vagina and rectum which leaves them unable to control leaking from the bladder and bowel. Fistulas may result in the isolation of a woman from family and friends when she can't keep herself clean and many women are divorced by their husbands when fistulas and the resultant smell make them undesirable.

Vinod and Caren began the long trip to Dubti but ran into an MSF staffer on the way. The staffer told them that the surgeon was on holiday from Dubti and the anesthesiologist was sick in Addis. They had to turn around and drive 220 kms in the opposite direction to take her to Desai, where she was delivered of a living child. The woman had been in labor for thirty hours including the bumpy and miserable five-hour drive. Nevertheless, Caren said the woman never cried out. She would flinch slightly when jolted but did not make a sound. Caren marveled at the stoicism. We told her that it was the norm for the Afar people. I had seen Vinod clean out horrid abscesses while the patient sat immobile. Only one kid had fussed when Milton was treating him in my presence and we used the best tranquilizer, a Dum-Dum lollipop that I had brought from the States. The kids didn't know what lollipops were but Milton told him "sucre," French for sugar, and he was quiet soon enough.

Another problem pregnancy presented while Vinod and Caren were away. Maria was called to a woman who was having seizures.

The pregnancy was very far along. She examined the woman and found edema in the hands and face and her blood pressure was high, making Maria suspect eclampsia. However, we could never forget about malaria. Maria asked me to do a smear for the parasites and the slide was positive for falciparum. But many of the Afar were positive for malaria without being severely ill. So was this cerebral malaria? Then I did the urinalysis that Maria had ordered. The patient had 3+ proteins in her urine; pretty diagnostic for eclampsia. The condition is found in roughly 5% of women in the US but is usually caught early, in the pre-eclampsia phase, during routine prenatal care. If it develops late in pregnancy, without treatment, it is most often fatal. The best treatment for eclampsia is delivery and we worried that there would be no surgeon available in Dubti to do a timely caesarian, if that proved necessary. Then we learned, via the radio, that Jean, the birder surgeon, was en route to Dubti to substitute for the surgeon who was on holiday. The patient was transported and got care. If MSF and our clinic had not been there, both this woman and the one already transported would almost certainly have died.

Help is coming to the Afar women. The Barbara May Memorial Hospital, a twenty-eight bed facility in Mille, the nearest village to Gahla, was at the time of this writing expected to open January 2011. The Foundation, funded by a group of Australian medicos and concerned donors, is particularly concerned about the women of the Afar region as it estimates that one in twelve will die from pregnancy and/or childbirth and thirty times that many will suffer damage.

Dr. Andrew Browning had been working with the Hamlin Fistula network, beginning 2001, and is now in charge of the regional Fistula Hospital in Barhir Dar in northwestern Ethiopia. Being intimately familiar with the obstetrical problems of the Ethiopian woman, he began the charity and, together with his aunt who is a nurse/midwife, Valerie Browning, has developed a three-tier system of maternity care. The initial step involves birth attendants who have been trained to recognize risk factors. If the attendant suspects a problem, she will send the woman on to a waiting area along the highway where trained Afar midwives will either deliver her or send her to the third tier, which is the hospital. The first Afar midwives have been trained by Valerie and will provide most of the staffing for the hospital with an additional expat obstetrician and an expat midwife who will handle emergencies and staff training. They have found a most worthy cause. The dangers of pregnancy and childbirth are probably to blame for the much lower life expectancy of the Afar woman, 47 years as opposed to 53 years for men. Both numbers are low due to the high number of deaths among infants and young children. The Child Mortality Rate (children under five) is a staggering twelve percent according to The Ethiopian Demographic and Health Survey, 2002. The Barbara May Foundation of Australia is paying for the equipment at the Mille Hospital, and it accepts donations.

We also had a drowning in mission, which would have seemed impossible in June when the river wasn't ankle deep. Now it was out of its banks and running with a powerful current. The river carried lots of branches and other detritus it had picked up on its way from the highlands. A man had fallen in, upriver, and the body was dragged out on our riverbank. No one knew who he was so the word went out for anyone traveling outside of Gahla to ask about anyone missing.

Small Victories

No one was starving in Gahla unless because of disease. I saw more hunger in Addis but Gahla was an artificial environment largely provisioned from outside. All it would take is one season without rain to destroy them. The Afar were totally dependent on their herds and if the herds could not get grass, everyone would suffer.

Nevertheless, we were making a difference right now. Ten-year-old Mariam, who had been bent over with TB of the spine, was upright after three months of treatment. She was often attended by her grandfather, who was obviously proud of her. Mariam had finished her first two months in the hospital tent and was now living with her family in the settlement and coming to the DOT tent (Directly Observed Treatment) tent daily. After they were released from hospital, patients could wander at will and I often saw Mariam and her grandfather walking by the river.

Vinod had treated a small boy for nephrotic syndrome. He came in swollen of body and face, whimpering with discomfort as he was unable to urinate. Just a short regimen of steroid treatment rid him of the water and, though he would remain with us for observation, he was able to join his siblings who had been staying with their parents in a small room adjacent to the hospital tent. The mother, who allowed me to photograph her, was without doubt one of the most beautiful women I have ever seen, a perfect blend of Caucasian and Negroid with her lovely oval face augmented with subtle tattoos above the brows, bridging the nose and circling in perfectly aligned arcs beneath the eyes.

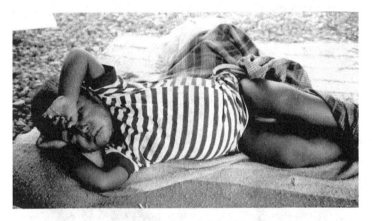

My job in the lab, though we had far more patients, up to fifty people being seen in one day, had become easier. Daoud, the last trainee, learned in a fraction of the time that poor Hammadou had struggled due to the fact that there were four others who could explain in his own language. It was a good thing as I no longer had the same energy. Both Aden and Daoud were family men and I hoped they could make some money with the skills they were learning.

Things were not so easy amongst the rest of the team. I came upon a shouting match between Maria and Fred. There was conflict over one of the Afar workers. I didn't know the background but Fred stayed behind after the argument. He told me that Jose had experienced trouble with the same man but Fred felt that Maria always blamed him. Fred was blamed for many things included the unvarying diet. Much of the blame was no doubt justified but I did commiserate with Fred, as he was so clearly miserable in his role. He had a fine mind as well as enormous curiosity. He told me that both of his siblings were professionals and I got the impression that Fred felt himself to be something of a disappointment. He was a classic case of talent in need of an outlet. I suggested that maybe he would like a different mission now that he knew what it was all about, but truly I could not see Fred building, wiring and plumbing. He was the ultimate people person. The photos he took were of himself with the Afar people, crouching with the children or standing with the Afar warriors, a stork among the diminutive Afar. He was still enamored of Zahra and there were still rumbles that her family did not appreciate it.

In truth, we were all sometimes bored. Though we saw a great panoply of conditions, it was the old "utter boredom interrupted by periods of sheer panic" routine. There was a long stretch between 11AM when we broke for lunch and 4PM when we started up again seeing patients. Vinod and I in particular lacked for reading material as the newspapers and magazines lying around the dining hut were in French. The only thing I understood were the political cartoons, the favorite subject being swaggering cowboy George Bush. I didn't need to read the caption to figure those out. I read all the medical texts in the office and a book I found about grizzly bears in Alaska. At least that one made me feel cooler.

Evidently, the high water was causing the snakes to move into drier areas. We had a family come in with their child who had been bitten on the hand. The parents had taken the child to a traditional healer first and the hand was hugely swollen now. We had no anti-venom, just as we had no blood grouping serums or HIV tests; the kerosene fridge would not keep any of those temperature labile items cool enough. Vinod used antibiotics since many snake bites don't cause systemic damage but do cause necrosis of the immediate bitten area. We all wished for a better way of cold storage. Had we needed a blood transfusion, there was no way for me to type the patient and the donor.

Moments to Remember

During the last week of August, Jean the birder surgeon came back with his wife, Caterine. She was the new Medical Director, since Dominique and Veronique had gone back to France, and a nurse by profession. Fred fixed dinner as Hammadini was again away. Caren, Maria and I moved out of our shelter so as to give them a place to sleep and we slept outside on mats in the courtyard. When I arrived in mission I would never have believed that I could sleep on the ground with no more padding than an Afar mat but sleep we did, just as the patients did in the hospital tents.

Maria had ordered mosquito nets for each patient bed, held up with a clever frame. They had not complained though their nets must have held the heat inside as much as ours. My new mattress had gotten wet within the plastic cover, presumably when the hard rains ran under the walls of our shelter. Since I no longer used my mat outside the door, I put my mat on the mattress and slept on that. I had rash on my arms, legs and back but I only had about ten days left of mission. I concentrated on other matters such as not leaving this area of the world that I knew few birders would ever visit without seeing every bird that could possibly be seen. I walked to the river one evening and just stood there marveling at the change wrought by water from the sky. What at first had been a narrow strip of dusty green along the river was now a wide swath and I had no doubt that in a few weeks, the wildflowers that Milton had mentioned (and which I had seriously doubted), would bloom as promised. While I stood there, a bird sailed out over the river. First I saw a black breast and back, rare enough as a plumage pattern, but it was set off with a snow white tail and the wings appeared, from my angle, an ice blue. After the bird was gone, I looked it up and found that it was a White-winged Tern. We do get White-winged Terns in the US as rarities but I will never see a White-winged Tern as I saw it that day, with the light tinting the feathers of the wings the way light diffracts the water in a swimming pool to make them appear blue. It reminded me of those pictures of angels with blue-white wings. I prefer the concrete world and White-winged Terns.

Maria, Caren and myself, along with Hiyu, had a morning out when Maria arranged for us to go to the little restaurant which had sprung up within walking distance of Gahla, presumably to take advantage of the money being made and spent in the area of mission. It was run by two highlanders and sold sundries and kaat as well as food, proving that entrepreneurship is worldwide. We had plain potatoes with a few lentils and dabo, but it was different; and we had coffee! I had taken to putting a little pan of water on the coals of the cook's fire in the morning and using the coffee bags my sister had sent me. It was obvious that the coffee habit had not died. It was only in remission.

More deboiters meant more kids and by now we had a soccer team. The boys loved to kick around a partially deflated soccer ball with Vinod, Jose and Fred providing expertise. I had to keep reminding myself to call it football. The girls ran around trying to get into the action but I never saw them with the ball. Maria and I had to remind our men to encourage equal rights.

In addition to the Mille restaurant, there was now a Central Hotel. The streets were still mud, the walls were made of cement blocks chinked with mud and the sign was a little delicate, being held up on a tripod of skinned saplings, but it was a sign of progress. All of us went over to sit on the patio and drink a Pepsi. The man at the next table had an infant Gelada baboon which he put down on the table for us to see. It knocked over my Pepsi and was sucking it off the tabletop thirstily. Caren told him that he must give it some milk and he said he would give it goat's milk, but we were afraid it would not live. The little thing climbed up my shirt and clutched at me like a human baby. Geladas have only one offspring at a time and I could imagine that this infant's mother did not give her child up willingly. The longing of the little male for his troop was clear in his dark eyes, humanlike and sad.

Two days before I left mission a highlander tech came from Addis to take over until the expat tech could arrive. His name was Samuel, an Amhar, and it was a real pleasure to meet him. I was surprised to learn that techs who study in Addis use the same textbooks used by tech students in the US. I had brought an atlas of cell morphology to mission and he noticed it immediately as one he had used. It was then that I realized why all higher education in Ethiopia required English. All the books were in that language.

I told Samuel about our difficulties with the centrifuge and my concern that we would not be able to identify Bilharsia. He told me that the way to do it is to use an old light bulb. Knock the screw end off so that it becomes a narrow necked flask which is then filled with urine to the very top. A slide is then placed across the neck and the flask is set in the sun. Samuel said that the larva of the Shistosomes come to the light and concentrate against the slide. The slide can then be removed after an hour or two and examined under the scope. I had wasted the time and energy of my trainees trying to spin urine down.

I visited the hospital tents for the last time on the afternoon of August 30 and got a picture of Oskar, the pitifully undernourished baby that had come in close to three months earlier. He had thrived on Maria's feeding regimen and TB treatment. He was a fat cheeked little fellow by this time and I was even able to coax a smile from him as he was held in his mother's arms. Oskar was worth a lot of sweating.

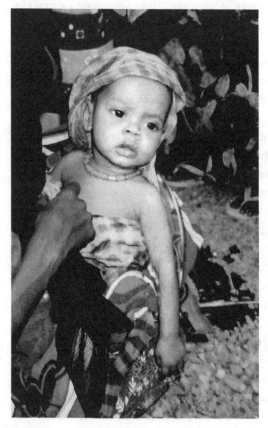

Unfortu-
nately, Samuel
did not speak
Afaraf or French.
Hammadou and
Adais were sent
to the lab to meet
him and I no-
ticed right away
that there was
reserve on both
sides. The divide
widened at din-
ner. The cook
had come up
with some bits
of meat for flavor
and Samuel did
not want to eat
any meat cooked
by a Muslim. We
assured him that
eating meat was
not going to be an issue other nights, but he stated with conviction
that he would only stay one month. He ate very little and seemed quite
ill at ease. If there is only one God, as most faiths attest, why is religion
so divisive?

Adais had undertaken to dictate a note to me which one of the staff
wrote for him. It was very touching as he expressed his "deep feeling on
missing me" and went on to say that "I wish you all the bests from the
bottom of my heart." He also asked me to send copies of the pictures
from Dubie Lake. That must have been a fun time for him. I wished
that I had received the note before I made the decision to leave him my
French-English dictionary. He appeared embarrassed when I gave it to

him. It was an ignorant move on my part because I should have realized that he couldn't read or write.

It was early in the day and the sputa were still being collected. Alone in the lab, I did the calculations that Laurence had requested involving number of slides stained versus number of positives, which demonstrated the 26% positive rate for direct smear. We had treated many patients for TB and many more could be expected to come. But had I really helped to save any lives? Maybe. The sad fact is that having TB and being cured does not confer lasting immunity as does measles. The same patients could get it again, or any number of other illnesses.

The only lasting change I could be sure I had made while in Gahla was the change in me. I had come full of do-gooder ideas and overconfidence but, having been given a healthy dose of realism, I now saw my contribution as a "drop in the ocean" (at best) of need. I now knew I would not save the world, but I also knew that I could never again be unaware of that world. I could only make my puny efforts and support the efforts of others, outside my door and outside my country. I carefully laid two extra positive slides that I had stained for Laurence into a slide holder as she had requested in order to show her the results of my staining method. There was no danger in carrying these smears as the organism is killed in the process of staining.

I then threw away my last mask, bleached the counters for the last time, took my pictures off the wall and left the cell atlas in the Gahla lab. I left my blue-edged natala on my mattress. I left the insect repellent and the sun screen for the team, and I left nearly all of my clothes. One day during my last week in mission I finally weighed myself and calculated from kilograms into English units. In my three months of mission, I had lost eighteen pounds.

CHAPTER 12. HOME, TO A CHANGING WORLD

On the last day of August, I left Gahla. The Afar were asking who was going to do their sputa, as some of them still remembered how it had been before the lab was up and running. I could assure them that good people would be in charge as I had complete confidence in Samuel and also in Hammadou, Adais, Aden and Daoud to stain and read. Just before I had to get in the land cruiser to leave, Fred came running up and gave me a giant hug that I knew was genuine. It was no easy thing to leave these people, once strangers, whom I had come to love. Maria and I sobbed. Vinod was accompanying me to Addis and Hassan as well. Hammadou went with us for part of the journey and kissed my hand when we said good-bye. I was in limbo for the first part of the journey as my thoughts were back in Gahla but my subconscious must have stayed aware, as I did come out of it when I spotted a Go-Away-Bird. The Go-Away-Bird eats fruits, flowers and buds and at nineteen inches it could probably pack away quite a few. It was probably named Go-Away by the farmers who didn't want to share, but it was a timely sighting for me. Later, I was blessed with the sight of a Bateleur, a striking bird of prey, black head and wing tips, large white wing patches and vivid brick-colored feet, bill and nape.

I saw a few new birds in Addis, the Red-eyed Dove for one, but it is fitting that the last bird I will mention is the Abyssinian Crimsonwing. I got it close to Addis, where the trees started. It wasn't the most beautiful Crimsonwing in the book, not one of the bright red ones or the one with the speckled breast. It was a smaller Crimsonwing, the body a dull olive. But the name was apt. I had birded at least some of Ethiopia with a total species count of one hundred-fourteen. Not so great out of a possible eight hundred, but I did see the Abyssinian Crimsonwing.

Dominique and Veronique were gone, of course. There was no more mention of going to the mission in western Ethiopia and I didn't bring it up. The spirit was willing but the flesh was very weak. When I saw myself in the mirror for the first time in several weeks, I could hardly believe my eyes. My face was a mass of wrinkles. I knew and Vinod assured me that the dehydration would right itself quickly under better conditions, but it was a shock nonetheless to look like my great-grandmother when she was ninety.

Gesign, a highlander nurse who had visited mission with Moussa, asked to accompany Vinod and me when we went to get our films developed. It was very convenient to have him drive us but he insisted on buying us some Ethiopian clothing, though we both tried mightily to dissuade him. I was well aware that his pay probably did not allow for this type of expenditure but he insisted, so I chose a cotton vest with the triangular design that I had often seen in Ethiopia.

Hassan, our native nurse, invited us to his home for dinner. Hassan told us, through an interpreter, that he was determined that we have one good meal before we left Ethiopia. Again, it seemed that he took it as an affront that the Western world thought Ethiopia was starving. We arrived at his home in the afternoon and were greeted by Chafika, whom I had met before and also by his wife, other daughter, and a young boy. An older boy was elsewhere. It was a roomy home and comfortable. A large cloth was laid on the floor of the living area and we all sat around it on low cushions and divans. Chafika entertained us with pictures of her parent's wedding, which was not the primitive "drag the bride kicking and screaming to her fate" wedding as broadcast on the Travel Channel. Instead I was once again impressed by the similarities in the wedding ceremonies of different cultures. I had seen pictures of the Asian wedding of one co-worker and the Hindu wedding of another as well as many Western weddings and this one involved the same concepts of dressing up, eating together and gifting the newlyweds. When dinner began in Hassan's house, so much food was brought that I can't begin to describe it. There were fresh salads and cooked vegetables including my beloved beets. There were savory meats similar to what we had when Aisha had the sheep killed. At the end we had the coffee ceremony. Chafika did a presentation of a farewell gift to me. It was an Afar wall hanging, made by the little boy, in traditional triangular motif. It was the perfect souvenir, having been woven of the same reeds that had sheltered me in the form of mats for three months in mission. I asked her what I could send them and she shyly asked for books. I also learned that her dad liked chocolate.

Gesign had also been invited. He told me he was Orthodox but it didn't bother him to eat Muslim food. He ate it with relish. Gesign was eager to come to the United States. He asked me about it often and I promised to send him information on getting his RN in the US, but I had grave misgivings about whether a job here would be the great thing he imagined it to be. He would definitely have made more money, but he was used to a very laid-back pace of working, not the non-stop and stressful nursing of the West. I also was concerned that he would experience racism. Milton told me early on, "One has to come to Africa to see Africans at their best." Upon reflection, I knew he was right. These Africans had no experience of being slaves, no rancor. I hated to think that Gesign might not be treated as well in my country as I had been in his.

At 10:30 PM on September 1, I left Addis Ababa. There was a moment of discussion when the X-ray of my luggage in Addis revealed my five Afar jiles, but when I explained that they were souvenirs, I was allowed to keep them in my checked baggage. Of course, I never doubted that they would sail through US customs though Vinod had not bought one as he said he would never get it into Australia. Those were the days of our innocence (or ignorance).

I took a cab at the Paris airport. Maria had warned me that the private cabs were expensive but the flight had been twelve hours long and I did not have the verve that I had possessed three months before.

Another trek through the multiple levels of the airport, toting luggage, was not in me.

Since I arrived on a Sunday, I could not check in at the MSF office. But on every corner was an ATM machine, so I was finally able to access the funds in my US bank account. I then found a type of discount store where I could buy underwear for myself and a pair of pants that did not fall off and some lotion which I used to begin the rehydration process. The rash was still with me. I learned that the young people in Paris speak English well and enjoy using it. The clerk at the store was very helpful and even used a picture from their ad layout to explain to me that I had bought enough to qualify for a bonus prize. It was a small alarm clock. I could only smile. For three months I had awakened to the call for prayer, to bleating goats and to the sounds of foreign tongues. I was back in the land of the alarm clock.

Coming through Paris on the way in, I had been too intimidated to cross the threshold of a real restaurant and had to settle for a gyro, two nights in a row. This time, I was determined to do better. The temperature was a refreshing 55F so I wandered in the area of Paris that I had come to know. I peeked in the window of a restaurant near the office of MSF and was able to puzzle out the sign for their special, or most of it, anyway. Fred would have been proud of me. Between my stumbling French and the English of my young and pleasant waitress, I was served some delicious Dorade, what we would call Mahi in a Florida restaurant, rice, salad and lovely chocolate gateau. Given the location, she probably got a lot of foreigners and I could have enjoyed the good French food during my sojourn three months earlier had I not been afraid. Why do we hesitate? We long for new experience, at the same time fear it, and then wind up learning that our needs as human beings are the same everywhere and it is a basic premise of humanity to help other beings meet those needs.

Debriefing

At the MSF office the next day, I was able to meet Françoise, the lab tech who would replace me at Gahla. She was very personable and seemed to understand my English well enough. She had been on mission before and I suggested that perhaps she would be better prepared to last the full length of time. She smiled and assured me that she had no intention of staying six months. I delivered the typed procedures that I had prepared and the slides to Laurence's office but was disappointed not to see her again, as she was out.

Nicholas told me that the box sent by my hospital in Florida had been detained by customs because there was a camera inside, a last minute addition by the techs there. I told him to just send the whole thing on as a donation to mission. I had written to ask for a manual diff counter, a device one uses to tabulate the various kinds of white blood cells. The techs had sent that item along with other equipment which was no longer used in their automated and computer driven lab. The techs and our pathologist were very supportive of mission.

I also met again with Isabel and apologized to be returning in only three months. Isabel assured me that they would rather have the three good months that I had given them than for me to be sick for three more. She told me that she and Anne-Louise agreed that Gahla had the toughest living conditions of any mission either of them had ever seen and they had seen plenty. She called in a co-worker who was in charge of equipment and we talked about the problems with the kerosene refrigerators. He kept repeating that the fridges had served them well and they had not had bad reports about them. I could only answer that perhaps the others weren't operating in 120 degree heat.

After debriefing, I had time to visit a bookstore. I wanted to buy some English language books to send back to Gahla. The clerk was middle aged and I feared that I would get that shake of the head that means the listener does not understand my language, but he immediately responded to my, "Do you have any paperbacks in English?" with a nod and showed me to a small pile of about six. Encouraged, I asked the price and got the whole pile for a small sum. I also found an anatomy chart for Hassan to use in teaching the APDA boys and some bangle bracelets for the kitchen girls. I took the package back to the office where I put it in the box for Addis, hoping someone would be going soon, perhaps Françoise. There were many things I would have liked to buy for those still at mission but I couldn't expect outbound volunteers to carry a lot of non-essential items.

It seems that most of the flights into and out of Africa are night flights, or perhaps MSF has found another way to save the money for where it will do the most good. I arrived in New York at 10AM on September 4. Isobel had e-mailed the MSF office in New York about my return but the two people she had mailed were not in so I was a total surprise, unexpected but certainly not unwelcome. The staff at MSF New York may not be the most organized of groups but they are without doubt one of the warmest. Due to the inflexibility of our system, it has been very hard for the New York office to get techs to volunteer, and many potential volunteers in all areas are prevented because they can't get time off or they can't pay their recurring bills on what was then a six hundred dollar stipend. Some want to take families along. MSF does not allow children to go on mission, a rule which, having experienced the hardships, I consider very wise. So the New York office cherishes the volunteers it is actually able to send. Juliet, after one look at my wasted body, ran out and bought me a huge slice of New York cheesecake, and it was great to sit with them and show them the pictures of Oskar and Miriam, cures about which we could all feel good. They got me a flight that same day and my brother picked me up at the Tampa airport at 11 PM that night.

I e-mailed to let the group know that I had arrived safely. The reply indicated that Vinod and Maria would also be leaving soon and that Fred was obliged to go home due to serious complaints in the Afar settlement about his relationship with Zahra.

Oblivious No More

It was exactly one week after my return from mission that I took a package to the post office containing the books that I was sending to Chafika and her sister, some Danielle Steele as she had requested but also some Nevada Barr, along with a big bag of M&Ms for Hassan. The clerk at the window, a naturalized Korean, saw the address in Ethiopia and asked, "Are the people in Ethiopia Muslims? " I was taken aback by the question but answered that yes, this family was. He frowned and shook his head. Later that day, as I was sitting on the floor of my home arranging the pictures from mission, the phone rang. My daughter advised me to turn on the TV as she knows I seldom watch it. I sat transfixed along with the vast majority of Americans as I watched the World Trade Center tumble down, first one tower and then the other, on every channel. They said Muslims were responsible. I watched Bin Laden with his message of hate and I could only think, "but not MY Muslims, not Adais or Hammadou or Sheik Ahmed or Kadir or the woman who fed me 'soup'." Muslim was the word of the hour, a dirty word. I listened to the militant reactions as I held the pictures in my hand, lovely Medina, the kitchen girls, Urdu and the children holding out their hands for tattoos. How could it be?

When I finally went to my computer that evening, there was a message from Samuel Kinde, the highlander tech, reproduced here:

DEAR MADAM JONES! ARE YOU OK?

Yesterday evening I heard the bad news; really I feel very sorry. It is our centuries biggest tragedy I ever hear in my life, early this morning everybody was asking about you, really they love you too much they call you every bodys' mother. We all feel sorry about the people who died of the accident and would like to say "May the Lord in the heaven bless their soul. AMEN."

dear jones, soon as I get your respons I will tell you everything about my current situation.

Wish you love from my bareheart, wish your country everlasting peace.

samuel kinde

Yes, Samuel was Christian but I know he spoke for everyone at mission. Those people did not hate Americans; at least, they didn't then. Since we did not satisfy ourselves with retaliation on the supposed location of Bin Laden but instead, for reasons that remain murky, chose a preemptive strike on an unrelated Muslim nation, a lot more people hate us now.

It took fifty-six years and the experience of living among the "other guy" to make me realize that it is just a very few people in any group who choose for their own reasons to be mouthpieces and who thereby hardwire the opinion of the rest of the nation about that group. In the eight years that have passed since 9/11, I have seen the United States become increasingly anti-Muslim. Last Christmas, I received the same e-card four times with the message that "Jesus is the reason for the season," entreating me to make sure everyone I meet is aware that Christmas belongs to the followers of Christ and that "America is a Christian nation." There is a billboard on US HWY 19 advertising the "No Separation" lobby, the members of which want to do away with the separation of church and state. They contend that the founding fathers used "Christian principles" when writing the US Constitution.

I graduated from a Catholic college. It was closest to my house and allowed me to pile on the extra courses free of charge beyond the first twelve credit hours. That college insisted that I take a religion course, a requirement which I bitterly resented. I chose The New Testament because it was offered at a time that fit into my schedule. I expected to suffer through it. My instructor had for ten years lived the life of a religious monk before leaving and deciding to marry. I expected him to preach the Catholic agenda but he disabused me of that preconception. He told us that it's OK to think, to question. When we found passages in the Bible that portray Jesus as abrupt and judgmental, he asked us if we thought those passages to be a realistic portrayal of Jesus. We all felt that some quotes were out of character. He told us that it probably didn't sound like Jesus because Jesus probably didn't say it. He didn't think that every printed letter of God's Word was God's word. It was written over centuries by men with "iffy" memories and questionable sources and, of course, their preconceived opinions. Ex-monk also pointed out that Jesus was not the first to come up with the Golden Rule. Confucius used it and the Hebrews and other ancient civilizations used it; and it really is just common sense. He taught the Bible as a compass, not a map. The founding fathers were mostly Universalists and they founded this country on time-honored principles that rely more heavily on the Romans and the Greeks than on the Bible. They separated church and state because they feared zealots, all kinds.

Sometimes bumper stickers tell it all, particularly the one that says "We're creating terrorists faster than we can kill them." It was with real disappointment that I read a *National Geographic* article (October

2005), entitled "The Cruelest Place on Earth, Africa's Danakil Desert." The author, Virginia Morell, writes of joining an Afar salt caravan with an Afar guide. First she tells of being prevented from continuing with the caravan after they meet up with one of the rebel groups, the Afar Revolutionary Democratic Unity Front, the members of which are not letting anyone through. They are still intent on getting back some land that they lost when Eritrea seceded from Ethiopia in the 1990s. Then she went on to say that, in this caravan, fifteen months after 9/11, she was appalled to find that many of the Afar were wearing T-shirts with Osama Bin Laden's image! It was particularly upsetting when their guide removed his outer shirt and displayed the same picture. When she asked him about it, the guide said she should not worry. They revered Bin Laden because he had struck a great blow against Satan in Allah's behalf. It had nothing to do with her or her country. There is definitely a disconnect there. Do they think they can hate the American government but not Americans? Does it mean that, given their reputation, they just like a good fight? Ms. Morrell's guide, Edris, is quoted as saying "In our history we have always been fighters. We live in the desert and because it's a hard land, we must fight, even though killing is against the will of Allah. And when we fight, we use whatever we have: guns and knives, rocks and sticks. We will even bite with our teeth. You use everything when you fight against your enemies." It sounds like maybe Osama is the Eric Rudolph of the desert. Rudolph was helped and hidden for years by people in the Smoky Mountains who did it because they could. Osama has probably become the same type of folk hero since, despite the two wars being waged ostensibly over his crime, he is still at large, a thumb to the nose at America and her resources.

So, to me, the question is, were the Afar in Gahla in sympathy with me over 9/11 because they knew me personally? The Afar, like the rest of Ethiopia, were definitely pro-American when I was there. Did the Afar turn against us when they started hearing all the anti-Muslim rhetoric? If it's the former, we'd better start getting ourselves out there, on a personal level, and dissociate ourselves from the tanks.

The purpose of this book is to speak of the people among whom I lived, not just the Afar but also the unsupported veterans and hungry children on the streets of Addis. I also speak for the Muslims who are not terrorists—and that is the vast majority of Muslims. Ethiopia was not a war torn population (as many are where MSF works). The family units had not been torn apart and we were not all in danger every day of enemy attack, at least not of the human kind.

MSF is still treating TB in other parts of Ethiopia and techs are still needed to stain and read smears for AFB until a better method comes along. PCR tests can detect TB quickly and with accuracy and can even detect drug resistance, but they require special equipment. Peter Small of the Bill and Melinda Gates Foundation, which has been funding TB research, said he is concerned that the potential high cost of such a sophisticated test might limit its use around the world and, of course, this equipment would require proper electric power. There is now a kit test in use for malaria. But the kits are expensive and the treatments for malaria and TB, for AIDS and all the rest, are also expensive. MSF constantly negotiates with drug companies to allow them to buy medicines at reduced prices. Their newest campaign, called "Europe! Hands off Our Medicine," focuses on the new threat of tougher intellectual property provisions than have been in use to date. The challenge is to the Indian Patents Act of 1970 that prevents "evergreening," the practice by pharmaceutical companies of making trivial changes to existing medicines in order to extend the periods of their patent, thereby stifling the generics market.

MSF gets 80% of its AIDS medicines from India, where they are made as generics. According to the MSF website, these meds keep 160,000 people alive every day. The trade agreement proposed between Europe and India could block the sale of these meds or even their production as Europe is, per the MSF press release, "also the driving force in the secret negotiations for an Anti-Counterfeiting Trade Agreement. Already, under EU customs regulations, legitimate generic medicines have been detained in European ports." Ten years ago multinational companies had a stranglehold on AIDS medicines due to patents. It has been the generics that have allowed MSF and other humanitarian organizations to treat HIV with success. That success has allowed parents with HIV to go on raising their children and to go on working so that those children will not be orphans without support. Unless the trade

agreements exempt the drugs needed in the developing world, if generic manufacture is made illegal, HIV/AIDS, which is now at the level
of a chronic disease in wealthy countries, will mean death within a few
years for the poor.

Why, you may ask, should MSF get meds at reduced prices when
there are people in the United States who can't afford their medicines?
I won't go into the economic structure involving the drug companies
who want to be repaid for their research and then some, on top of their
overall high profitability, or the failure of government to insist on discounts for high volume purchase of medicines such as Medicare and
Medicaid should be enjoying. In this country we do have recourse to a
social catch system, to Medicaid, to drug company discount programs,
to our own savings. The people among whom MSF works have none of
these. The Afar people have goats, camels and pride. They do not have
cash, doctors, medicines or government help.

Just a few months after I came home from mission, the UN Emergency Unit for Ethiopia was obliged to do an assessment mission of the
Afar region covering May 29–June 8, 2002. The rainy season had not
been adequate and the report includes several pictures of camel car-
casses and dying cattle. The report mentions increased conflict with
the Issa, who, it says, are well armed and known for their "gun running
and contraband merchandise." The Issa want to establish control of the
Awash river bank and of the main road to Addis and Djibouti. That area
has belonged to the Afar, and the Awash green belt is the only fertile
land in all the Afar region. The Afar were trying to defend their territory at the same time they were undergoing a drought. Milk sales in
the only co-op in the region had fallen from forty liters during a normal
rainy season to just ten liters. Hungry and thirsty goats were not able
to provide enough milk to feed the owners' families. There was none to
sell. Since the wealth of an Afar is measured in livestock, Afar men often
wait to sell their animals, hoping for better times, until the animals are
emaciated. When they are forced to try to sell them, they bring little or
nothing. Even salt production has met with competition and the Afar
are falling back on charcoal making, taking trees that anchor the soil
and provide animal food. The Afar Pastoralist Development association
is mentioned in the UN report as having constructed water ponds in

the driest regions. The Afar are trying to help themselves, but it is an uphill battle and a very high hill.

I heard from several sources that I would never be the same after I had gone on mission. This is true. I cooked a twenty pound turkey for Thanksgiving last year, not because there were many to feed but because it was so cheap, 49 cents/ lb. for enough meat to feed the entire staff at Gahla, expat and native alike. I often hear it said that, "We can't feed them all," or "They need to stop having babies." Yes, I realize that we can't feed the world and there are too many children born into families without resources. But I found the figure of 3% on several different web sites. America's foreign aid program amounts to 3% of the amount we spend on our military. By midyear 2010, we had spent $1 trillion dollars on the wars in Iraq and Afghanistan, per the Congressional Report, much of it going to private contractors who are seldom held accountable for what they do; they do not follow codes of conduct or answer to the same justice as the US military is meant to do. At the same time, we have given a $1.5 billion in aid to Afghanistan and another billion to Pakistan. Has it brought us their respect or loyalty?

American Friends Service Committee, AFSC, likens the trillion dollars to giving each one of 15.3 million US adults who are out of work the sum of $50,000 each with $235 billion left over. For another perspective, AFSC has calculated that for the amount we are spending in just one day of the war, we could have: placed 95,364 children in Head Start, funded 163,525 people with health care, provided 6,482 families with homes, hired 12,478 elementary school teachers and given 34,904 four year college scholarships. So why aren't we doing that?

The simple answer is the lucrative weapons trade. For weapons and munitions to continue to be sold, weapons and munitions must be used. In October 2010, the US made a $60 billion arms sale to Saudi Arabia, a country we have long courted and which we, together with others, have made rich via oil revenues. If we say that some Saudis are funding and training Muslim terrorists, is this wise?

The US military budget accounts for 46.5% of the world's total military budget. We are even using our military to deliver aid in the same areas where we are fighting wars. In a *Washington Post* article (Nov. 18, 2008), George Rupp, President of the International Rescue Committee, says that "during the past decade, the Pentagon's share of the US over-seas development assistance budget has grown from 3.5% to 18%." The US and its partners channel much of their aid dollars through Provin-cial Reconstruction Teams, military groups who oversee military and civilian activities in international conflict zones. This has resulted in confusion to the local people who do not know whether we are friend or foe and also has endangered outside aid workers who may be mis-taken for military.

When I look at these figures, combating hunger doesn't sound so expensive. And, by the way, the term used now by the World Food Program and in US government programs is not "hunger." It is "food insecurity," which in a way may sound like a euphemism but at the same time it expresses the reality that a nation that has trouble feeding its population is, in fact, facing a security threat. It would seem that we could eliminate a lot of food insecurity with just a small relocation of the military budget.

The US is not the only national entity using foreign aid to enrich its own citizens. Paul Valley wrote in *The Independent* (London, Nov. 26, 2003)[9] that the West in general spends 30 times more on domestic farm subsidies than it does on aid. Nutriset, the French company making Plumpy Nut bars, has filed for patent protection on the concoction. Other nations feel that patent protection on Plumpy Nuts bars will interfere with similar formulations that could be made by local pro-ducers closer to the area where they are needed. Self-protection knows no national boundaries but we, as citizens, can insist that our nation sends adequate aid. A study conducted by MSF among 500 children in Niger showed that more than twice as many fed with CSB, the blend using US grain, required hospital treatment than those using RUTFs (Ready to Use Foods) which provide nutrients in concentrated form. The World Food Program confirms that the challenge is the capacity to make and fund RUTFs so that younger children can have access to this better food intervention. Our own children in the US are suffering obe-sity. It has been suggested that the widespread use of High Fructose Corn Syrup is one of the reasons. Taxpayers are heavily subsidizing the

---

9 Reprinted in *World Hunger, op. cit.*

corn used for that syrup. Perhaps we are also being fed food of lower quality because it benefits agricultural interests.

Americans are a generous people. Witness the outpouring for Haiti. I said as much to the Italian-American doctor with whom I rode to mission and his response was, "Yes, but they can afford to be." Perhaps, but most of those who give could instead find something they want or even need for themselves with that money. In the United States we are so busy earning our keep (as we work more hours than almost any other nation), we don't have time to follow up to see whether the money was put to its best use.

There are other political impediments as well. The US government naturally has to work through the governments of the nation involved, when offering help, and there is all too often a ruling clique with its own interests to serve, or a suspicion that precisely those aid workers will bring in military personnel that are hard to get rid of. And then, there are transportation and logistics problems beyond our comprehension.

The Quakers say, "There is that of God in Every One." For the agnostics among us, that can be paraphrased with the addition of one letter, "There is that of Good in Every One." It makes it so much simpler if we don't have to sort out which God. The best NGO's are those with no hidden agendas. From the article "About MSF: The MSF role in emergency medical aid," we read

> In carrying out humanitarian assistance, MSF seeks also to raise awareness of crisis situations: MSF acts as a witness and will speak out either in public or in private about the plight of populations in danger for whom MSF works. In doing so, MSF sets out to alleviate human suffering, to protect life and health and to ensure respect for the human beings and their fundamental human rights.

> Only a small percentage of the populations that find themselves in a situation of danger gain the attention of the media. MSF teams travel to places that many people have never heard of, to assist those who have fallen victim to natural or man-made disasters. MSF volunteers have a story to tell when they return from their missions, and they use their experiences to speak on what they have seen. For MSF, raising awareness for these populations and the situations they are in, is an important task.

I've been asked if I would ever go on mission again. I married Merle Hubbard in 2003. We have a combined family and I still work part-time at three area hospitals. But I would if I could. Vinod and I felt the same about mission. We may have been physically miserable but we were alive every day. We were not worrying about malpractice. We were using our talents and stretching our horizons. It was a real adventure, an education, and hey, those birds!

MSF left Gahla in 2005 and the remaining patients there were transferred to the national TB program. But treatment continues in other missions and there is no end to need.

I was not able to keep in touch with Samuel as Maria had the satellite phone taken out before she and Vinod left mission; another cost saving but at the loss of e-mail. I have lost touch with most of my team but there is not a day that I don't think of them and of the patients. At one time I took yoga classes at the Jewish Community Center near my home. There was a sampler on the wall with a proverb I have never forgotten, "One good deed is worth a thousand prayers." Whoever first advanced that idea was a kindred spirit. It seems to me that the effect of good deeds is easier to quantitate. And besides, where's the excitement in prayer?

The author
at her scope
in Gahla

INDEX

A

Abyssinia, 130
Acid Fast Bacillus (AFB), 32, 34, 55, 166
Action contre la Faim, 26
Addis, 7-10, 12-13, 15-16, 19, 39, 43-44, 47-48, 53, 55, 58-60, 64-66, 69, 74-75, 77, 91-97, 99-101, 106, 108, 110, 112, 115, 117-118, 126, 129, 135, 144-146, 148, 153, 157-159, 161, 166-167
Afar, 6, 14, 19-20, 22-24, 27, 31-32, 34-35, 37-39, 41-45, 47, 52-54, 56-67, 69, 71-74, 76-77, 79-81, 85-86, 89, 91, 96-97, 105, 107, 109-110, 112-114, 117, 119-123, 125-137, 139, 141, 145-151, 157, 159, 162, 165, 167-168
Afar Liberation Front, 135
Afar National Democratic Movement, 135
Afar Sea, 121
Afar Triple Junction, 121
Afaraf, 22, 32, 114-115, 134, 154
AK47, 112
Aksum, 130
American Friends Service Committee (AFSC), 168
Amhar, 13-14, 93, 128, 153
APDA (Afar Pastoralist Develop-ment Association), 20, 40, 128, 161
Arms Sales to Africa, 112-114
Ascaris, 55
Australopithecus afarensis, 96
Awash River, 58, 121, 167

B

Bacille-Koch, 69
Barbara May Memorial Hospital, 147
Bilharziosis, 91
Bonte, Laurence, 3, 7
Borlaug, Norman, 142
Browning, Valerie, 128, 147
Bush, George, 63, 99, 151

C

Child Mortality Rate, 148
Chlamydia trachomatis, 49
Corn-soya blend (CSB), 97, 100-101, 169
Cryptosporidia, 55
Cushite(s), 129

D

Dabo, 74, 152
Danakil, 22, 85, 125, 129, 132-133, 137, 165
Deboiters, 31, 60-61, 80, 106-107, 139,

173